TALKING GLASGOW

'A wee nyaff' down for the 'fitbaw' battle between 'weers'
and the 'Aul Enemy'. (page 80)

TALKING GLASGOW

Albert Mackie

Illustrations by
John MacKay

BLACKSTAFF PRESS

ISBN 0 85640 169 2

Printed in Northern Ireland by The Northern Whig Ltd.

Contents

'He went oot when murra brurra cam in.'

Stanley Baxter and Billy Connolly have made the world aware that Glasgow has a language of its own, as remote from Standard Scots as from Queen's English. I call it Glescaranto. Here is a classical story (almost as ancient as the dialogues between St Patrick and Ossian) illustrating the social and linguistic background which inspires the humour of these and other comedians as well as a host of newspaper and magazine writers:

A 'dressed lady' went up a 'close' (the passage leading to the stairs in a tenement), by-passed the 'dunny' (back passage), and went up 'ra sterrs' and 'alang a loaby,' where she knocked at a door. After a painful interval, the door opened a creak to reveal the 'feart, peely-wally' (frightened, pale) face of a small boy. The following conversation ensued, the dressed lady speaking Standard English, which denizens of such a tenement would call Panloaf, Kelvinside, Big Hoose or Weel Pitten-On, while the child answered in Glescaranto, the peculiar Scots-English of many Glaswegians, and the one which comics and writers like to convey in amusing phonetics:

'May I speak to your father, sonny?'

'Oh, my farra went oot when ma murra cam in.'

'Then perhaps I could see your mother.'

'Naw, she went oot when ma brurra cam in.'

'Oh well, I'll have a word with your brother.'

'He went oot when murra brurra cam in.'

'Dear me! May I see your other brother?'

'Naw, he went oot when Ah cam in.'

'Isn't there anyone in the house I can talk to?'

'Oh, issiz no ra hoose, missiz, issiz ra cloazit.'

(This is not the house, madam, this is the shared W.C.)

The only thing really improbable about that old story is that the convenience still had its door. At one time, it is recorded, the closet on the landing could be shared by five homes and anything from twenty-five to fifty persons, and its introduction to Glasgow backlands was considered an improvement in its day. Nowadays, although Billy Connolly still sings 'Ah'm feart tae go tae the lavat'ry', these conditions are remote from the experience of a working-class living in high-rise and other modern flats, but they remain strong in racial memory.

Nor will the phrase 'dressed lady' convey much to a generation in which social workers are often not so well dressed as their cases.

One thing the story illustrates is the cavalier treatment of *th* in Glasgow's peculiar dialect. Mother, father, brother, other become 'murra', 'farra', 'brurra', 'urra'. The late Duncan Macrae sang, in his own version of 'The Wee Cock Sparra', 'Ra man hit ra boy, ro he wiznae his farra'. (The man hit the boy though he wasn't his father.)

'Ra' for 'the' is an infantile pronunciation carried into adult life by lazy speakers. When we were young we played a game in which we divided the confectioner's window and its goodies amongst us, and each of us claimed proudly (and yearningly) 'Aw raim's mine'. (All these, or them, are mine.)

When a humorously disposed Glaswegian (and there are many such) paints 'Raboa' on the bows of his speedboat or 'oarin' boat', he is caricaturing both this treatment of *th* and the glottal stop which afflicts the letter *t* in the middle or at the end of a word. Older Glaswegians spoke a more vigorous Scots in which the *t* was often emphatically pronounced, but now a hiatus or a choke has taken its place. When a Glasgow man says 'He's no a polis — he's a poul'ice' (not a policeman but a poultice) it is sometimes difficult to distinguish the two words.

It is this glottal stop which makes Glescaranto difficult to render phonetically in the manner of Hugo's modern language series or Sir James Wilson's *Dialects of Central Scotland*. Even in the spelling 'raboa' for 'the boat', the checking of breath which takes the place of the *t* is not adequately presented. It would require a special letter.

While older Glaswegians might still say 'Doon the watter' (down the River and Firth of Clyde) as if it really had 'twa t's', Glescarantists say, 'Doonra waa'er'. And if you said anything about a glottal stop they would suggest you were 'needin' yer heid luckt' (requiring your head to be examined — by a 'trick cyclist', or 'heid shrinker', of course).

When I started my newspaper career in Glasgow in 1928, I had to call at the surgical out-patients' department of the Infirmary for a check-up on an old injury. In the waiting room I sat beside a teenager (though we did not use that word in those remote days). He was a typical Gorbalonian of that period in monkey jacket, double-breasted waistcoat, Oxford bags and pointed patent-leather shoes. His head was bandaged like a mummy's or the Invisible Man's. A nurse came in and, saying, 'Ah've goat tae be cruel tae be kind,' proceeded to tear bandages and dressings rapidly off his badly slashed face. Plucky as he may have been in the encounter which left him with these ghastly cuts, he howled the place down and shed tears at the nurse's action. When she had gone and the howls had subsided, I asked the lad how he had got into this condition. All he said was, 'Ah was daunerin' owre Jamaica Brig on ma ain an' a coupla fluhs taen me fur anurra fluh.' (I was strolling across Jamaica Bridge on my own and a couple of fellows took me for another fellow.)&

In other parts of Scotland we might say 'fellie', but in Glasgow a male person is a 'fella', or 'fulla', usually telescoped to 'fla' or 'fluh'. It is this telescoping of words which makes Glescaranto strange to the ears accustomed to good diction.

Another time I was at an inter-city boxing match between Glasgow and Edinburgh. An Edinburgh boxer was knocked out in the second round, although he was the superior boxer. A young Glasgow boxer sitting beside me outside the ropes commented unemotionally, 'He's no a vruh strang fluh' (he's not a very strong fellow). 'Verra' for 'very' receives the same sort of treatment as 'fella'.

Strangely enough, Glaswegians hold on to long vowels as well as swallowing short ones. Theirs is a drawling speech, often musical, and it is impossible to convey in print the cadences of their sentences, which start high and finish low like musical phrases. As a child I was taught to say 'Doon the Clyde on the Clutha' in the Glasgow intonation, as if learning the tones of Chinese or the ups and downs of Norwegian.

A young Frenchman visiting my daughter recently in Dumbreck listened respectfully to a Billy Connolly L.P., and at the finish claimed he had understood most of it but admitted he was defeated by one word — 'What is "nat"?' he asked. 'Nat' (and that) is Billy Connolly's way of saying etcetera or 'and so on and so forth'.

'What did you have for your dinner?'

'Soup, nat, an' totties an' minsh, nat, an' some kinna pudden, nat.' (Soup and that, and potatoes and mince and that, and some kind of pudding and that.)

An old colleague and respected friend of mine, the late Councillor John S. Clarke, former M.P. for Maryhill, lion-tamer, archaeologist, journalist, Labour editor and president of the Scottish Burns Club, told me the following piece of Glasgow folklore:

When Quintus Lollius Urbicus was busy building the Antonine Wall between Forth and Clyde in the year 142 A.D., he was greatly harassed by

'At's aul Sneezer's fancy wumman so it is.'

the activities of a pygmy tribe called the Hellarii who menaced the western end of the wall. The Romans had named these little people from their habit of leaping up to look over the whin bushes (gorse) and crying, 'Whaur ra hell are ye?'

These tribesmen were not only a pain in the gorget to the legionaries but also a constant pest to the peace-loving Romanized Britons of Strathclyde, who called them 'Wee Nyaffs' and took care to have nothing to do with them.

Their principal cause of annoyance to the Romans was their habit of stealing bits of the wall, so that the Clyde end was never being properly finished, and also daubing the wall with slogans in spray-paint such as 'Gers furra Cup', 'San Toy rules O.K.' and 'We arra people' (which gave rise to yet a third name for the tribe, the Arrow People, though in fact their principal weapon was a razor).

Their depradations were making the contract with Antoninus Pius very difficult to complete on time and Quintus Urbicus was beginning to worry about his Lollius, but when he complained to the Emperor, all he could get from Antonine was an angry 'Surely such pygmies cannot defy the might of the Roman Legions. If you cannot extirpate these tribes, then at least capture some of them and send them to Rome that I, Caesar, may see what manner of men these are who set our Imperial power at nought!'

How their capture was effected the legend does not make clear, but two of the tribe, Wee Shooey and Wee Eck, were eventually transported in chains to Rome and brought before the Emperor, who laughed at the sight of them and ordered them to be thrown to the lions. Came the day when they were brought out from their cells and stood side by side in the arena of the Colosseum awaiting the release of the ferocious man-eaters. Looking down on them were Caesar and his entourage, including some of the most beautiful courtesans in all Rome.

Sharpening his razor on the sole of a patent-leather shoe, Wee Shooey said to Wee Eck:

'See aul Sneezer up err?'

'Wha?'

'Ra Tally Emp'rur, like.'

'Aw him? Ah jist caw um Tony. Whit aboot um?'

'See at dame alangside um? At smassher wirra rid herr. Up err in a nixt cherr. At's aul Sneezer's fancy wumman so it is.'

'Whit aboot it?'

'Well, at's whit Ah'm gonny tell ye. Las' night she cam shassyin' in tae see me. Ah wiz in ma cell — in masel, d'ye get it?'

'Ach, cut oot ra rotten jokes an' get oan wirra story!'

'Keepra heid, Mac! She says tae me, "Move owre, will ye?" an' she taks aff her sannies.'

'Wizzat aw she taen aff?'

'Gie's a chance tae tell a story! She taen aff aw rat Barralan joolery she's got roon her neck and roon her erms, nat.'

'Aw, get oan wi' it, fur oany favour!'

'She sterts tae let her herr doon tae her shoothers an' — Here ra lions, but! Ah'll tell ye efter!'

'The hauf o' yiz'll huv tae come down oot of there.'

A crowd gathers in Jamaica Street. Already we hear the whine of the ambulance:

'Whiss wrang, Mac?'

'A flaflaffalarry.'

This is a classical piece of Glasgow dialogue, at least fifty years old. The conversation went: 'What's wrong, Mac?' 'A fellow fell off a lorry.'

Now it would be:

'A flaflaffalangveekill.'

I spoke to a man leaning on a shovel over a hole in the road:

'Thassa rerr joab yiv goat, Mac.' (That's a good job you've got.)

'Yer kidneys.'

Had I not been a fluent Glescarantist, I'd have thought he was warning me about someone behind my back. But I knew what he was really saying was: 'Ye're kiddin iz.' In other parts of Scotland besides Glasgow, 'iz' (us) means 'me'.

With the big bands and the dance halls in the twenties and thirties, when we were denizens of the 'Denizen' (the Dennistoun Palais), Green's or the Albert, came the conversational gambit:

'Ye dancin?'

'Ye askin?'

'Whidgie hink?'

'Aw right well.'

'Smaashin flerr, intit?'

'D'ye c'meer oafen?'

'Seeza sherr urra flerr err.'

(Are you dancing? Are you asking? What do you think? All right then. Splendid dance-floor, isn't it? Do you come here often? Give me a share of the floor, you!)

The last remark was addressed to another male dancer.

'Seez' is common Scots for 'Give me' or rather 'Help me to' — really 'See iz', with again that 'iz' meaning 'us' but more usually 'me'. (It has been said that the only persons entitled to describe themselves as 'we' are an editor, a monarch and a man with fleas, but we Scots, while we'd never think of saying 'we' for 'I', often say 'us' for 'me'. Perhaps it is a split personality.)

An 'Aulfarran' (old-fashioned) Scot might say: 'Rax me a spaw o' yon bubblyjock!' (Reach me a foot, or leg, of yonder turkey-cock), but a Glaswegian of today would rather say: 'Seez owre at bit, ra turkey's fit!'

A Glasgow girl who had worked in London was asked how she managed to speak English so that the people in the South could understand her. She laughed:

'Och, 's easy! Ye jist cut oot aw the R's an' gie the wurrds a bit chow in the middle.'

That is nothing to what many Glaswegians do to their mother tongue. They extend the 'Bit chow' to the ends as well as the middle of the words and, although they tend to drawl slowly and gently and give the R's an extra kettledrum roll, they swallow a good many of the letters, or leave them to the imagination. The funny thing is that, through time, you not only understand them instantaneously, you find yourself talking like them.

Glasgow's atmosphere is impregnated, not only with petrol and diesel fumes, but also with puns inspired by the peculiarities of the language. Two cronies meet up town — 'two urra boays', you might say· — and immediately 'ra paa'er' begins:

'D'ye fancy ra Sarry Heid?' (Saracen's Head pub in the Gallowgate, famous for its cider.)

'Sowre faur.' (It is too far.)

'Well, Amphora.'

'Whidgie mean, Amphora?'

'Amphora bevvy — a hauf 'na heavy.'

(I am for a bout of drinking — a nip of whisky and a heavy beer.)

Every schoolboy knows that an amphora is an ancient two-handled vessel with a narrow neck, usually of earthenware, or, as we say, 'delf', 'jaury' or 'wally'. But to Glescarantists it immediately suggests an idea for a gag, and as it happens to be the name of an uptown pub, it's a 'brammer' (good one).

Just like the one about the young chap who went for an audition.

'What do you sing?'

'"Rappelle".'

13

'Don't know it.'

He starts to sing: 'Rappelle moon wiz shinin...'

Another offered the O'Hara song.

'How does it go?'

'Deep in O'Hara Texiss...'

But even when they don't chew the words, you find they have a different meaning. Take 'hurl', for instance. 'Ah'll hurl ye hame' doesn't mean you will be shot home from a circus cannon or a giant catapult. It means you will be given a lift, and possibly handled quite gently.

The senior citizen enjoying her bus-fare concession is asked: 'Whaur ye gaun, hen?' and replies: 'Ah dinnae ken yit, Ah'm only oot fur the hurl.'

When a city newspaper put out the poster in wartime: 'Germans Hurled Back', an old wife exclaimed indignantly: 'Hurled Back? Ah'd 'ae made the beggars walk.'

A popular song of fifty years ago was 'Ah loast ma hurl in the barra' (I lost my trip in the barrow) and the boy with 'a bone anarra' who let fly as the 'sparra' in the late Duncan Macrae's song, hit a man 'that wiz hurlin a barra' (pushing a barrow).

Some words are much more innocent in meaning than they sound. A case in point is 'tart', which, when applied to a woman in London, means a member of the oldest profession. But in Glescaranto it means a girl, with no reference whatever to her way of life.

I experienced this myself when I took two ladies — a well-known teacher of ballet and a respectable married friend — into a pub for a drink. I seated them in a corner and went up to the bar. Two working men were conversing with their sentences liberally punctuated with the non-U expressions some use to give more rhythm to their speech. One of them said quietly to the other: 'Keep the language doon! Thur a cuppla tarts sittin owre err.'

My experience corroborated, or at least made plausible, the story I had heard of a chairman of a smoker who had announced: 'Noo, lads, here a rale treat fur yiz. Oor nix singer is a young skill-teacher fae Auchenshoogle Acaudemy. Noo gie ra wee tart a big haun!'

This was the same man who later rebuked his audience for putting their fingers in the corners of their mouths and whistling shrilly for an encore: 'Ah shouldnae huv fur tae tell yous gents that artisses is nut dugs fur tae be whiss=lt at.'

I must not give the impression that all Glasgow people speak alike. Although originally it was a Lanarkshire town in which broad Scots was spoken, its classrooms teach through the medium of Southern or Standard English. In addition to this, since the Industrial Revolution, in which its working population was drawn largely from the Highlands and from Ireland,

'Noo gie ra wee tart a big haun!'

it has become the most Celtic of Scottish cities. Many of its inhabitants scorn to speak anything but English and at the same time the original native Scots tongue has become heavily infected with both English and Irish usages.

Although we always said 'is' or 'hiz' for 'us' and 'me', the word 'yiz' for 'you' seems to be an Irish importation, and I have sensed its spread across Scotland from the West to the East in my lifetime. We always said 'hiz yins' (us ones) but 'yous yins' is a quaint mixture of Anglo-Irish and Scots.

Not only do all Glaswegians not speak alike, but the same person will frequently switch from one dialect to another, according to company. This was the case with the bus conductress who changed to English in mid-sentence when she scolded some High School boys who had piled on to the top deck: 'The hauf o' yiz'll huv tae come down out of there.'

To the Glasgow tongue one word comes as easily as another. One hears 'our', 'oor' and 'wur' —'oors' and 'weers' for 'ours'. The chairman of a smoker I attended, in which workers from G. & J. Weir Ltd participated, got a laugh by announcing: 'You've heard the phrase: "One of ours"; well, the next turn is "Two of Weir's".'

The same people will use the Scots word 'yin' for 'one', and also the Anglo-Irish, or Highland 'wan'. We say, 'It's aw yin and wan' (one and one) to convey: 'Six of one and half-a-dozen of the other.'

Over-enthusiastic champions of Standard English, as opposed to Scots or any of its Glasgow variants, tend to talk what is locally called 'Kelvinside' — an injustice to one particular residential district. This is typified in the words of an old student song of Glasgow University — 'The fairies are dencing in the West End Perk.' In Edinburgh this 'fency' way of speaking is called 'Morningside'. Other cities have its equivalent. In London I have heard it called 'Kensington Hay'.

Glasgow people often imagine that Edinburgh people are inclined to talk an affected Panloaf. A Glasgow man at a football match thought the stranger standing next to him was talking rather 'perjinkly', and it naturally led him to ask:

'Are you frae Embruh?'

The other replied, as if speaking with a 'bool in the mooth' (a marble in the mouth):

'Naw — Ah cut ma mooth oan a boa'ull.'

Actually the majority of Edinburghers speak, if anything, more Scots than Glaswegians, and now, owing to the influence of Glasgow actors and comedians, especially on TV, they are beginning to talk like their Clydeside opposites.

The Glasgow tongue is highly infectious — both in its words and in its soft, musical lilt.

Very soon the conversational phrases trip easily off the non-Glaswegian's tongue:

'Hae oany o' ye oany oan ye?'

(Have any of you any on you? — An old man asking his friends for 'spunks' — matches.)

'Yaffa yatt? Whit yatt yaffa?'

(Are you off a yacht? What yacht are you off? — Wee smasher from Glasgow on holiday in Dunoon, to young man wearing a white-topped yachting cap.)

Master these and you will feel competent to sing 'Ammonia':

'Ammonia stro-olling va-a-gabaun...'

One old Scots word has remarkable currency in Glasgow speech and is interesting as an example of how words evolve in meaning. It is 'wally', which originally meant large and handsome, but two hundred years ago was being used by 'cadgers' (hawkers) to denote large and handsome ornaments sold to decorate the shelves of their customers — 'Bonnie wallies'!

As most of them were earthenware, 'wally' became the everyday word for china ('cheeny') and other glazed clay products. In Glasgow it developed even more sophisticated meanings. A 'wally close' in the city is a stair entrance with ceramic tiled walls, considered more than a cut above a close with painted and distempered walls.

'Wally dugs' (china dogs) are the best-known of the 'aulfarran' mantelshelf ornaments.

'Peely-wally' (sickly), used especially of children who are not thriving too well, may have been suggested by china ornaments on which the painting and glazing had peeled, revealing white patches like blanched cheeks.

But the most characteristically Glaswegian of the uses to which the word is put is 'wallies' meaning dentures. As the Poet Laureate of Paisley Road West, Scotland's answer to Sir John Betjeman, has put it:

'An aul wife went tae her doactur
   Wi a blush aw owre her face,
For she had a big shuge bealin
   Oan a kinna ridicklus place.

'"Whit happened?" asked the doactur.
   She answered, "Ah'm feart tae tell:
As Ah wiz lowpin owre ma bed,
   Ah went an' bit masel."

> ' "Ye muss be a coantoartionist
> Tae dae a thing sae gallus."
> "Dinnae be daft!" the aul wife said:
> "Ah jist sat doon oan ma wallies." '

Listening to Glasgow conversation, you wonder who all these people are they are talking about: Noah, Nora and Nat. 'Nat' you have already met as Billy Connolly's word for 'etcetera' — 'and that'. But you hear a lot also about 'Noah Chance', 'Noah Hoapinhell', 'Noah Derrsay', 'Nora Same', 'Nora Wanamean', 'Nora Hingataw' and 'Nora Weytaedaet'.

If you hear two porters chanting 'Noo yoo poo' and 'Poo yoo noo', they are not immigrants from Hong Kong. They are only saying, 'Now you pull' and 'Pull you now'!

Although 'bairns' is the word for children throughout Scotland, and in Glasgow it pops up with the pronunciation 'berrns', a much more frequently heard expression is 'weans', pronounced 'wanes'. Another of those old exercises in conversational Glescaranto went:

'Hud ra wane urra bashum!'

'Hold the child till I bashum!' — Supposedly spoken by a fond mother handing over her baby to get a good swipe at her man.)

'Ur thae wanes aw yours, or izziss a picnic?' the conductress asked the woman with the squad of children, to be told: 'Thur aw mines, an' it's nae picnic.'

'If Ah hudduv kent Ah wid nivveruv went.'

'Is your mother in, sonny?'

'Naw, she's went tae the supermarket.'

'Oh, laddie, where's your grammar?'

'*She's* went alang wi' her.'

This use of 'went' is the most frequent example of bent grammar in Glasgow. It is common enough in other cities and in the countryside as well, but it seems to stick out like a sore thumb in St Mungo's Dear Green Place.

Shakespeare used it, and if that fact was spread around it might stop the Glaswegians from using it. In Shakespeare's time 'went' was still part of the verb 'wend' — 'I wend, I went, I have went'. In those days Scots were saying, 'I gae, I gaed, I haif gane.'

Perhaps they were corrected when they said in English, 'I goed.'

'What's wrong with "I wish I hadn't goed", Johnny?'

'Please, miss, it should be "Ah wish tae Goad Ah hudnae went".'

Many of our grown-up acquaintances, as well as a lot of children, seem to miss no opportunity of coming away with this one.

'I thought this pub had go-go girls.'

'So it hud, but noo they've went-went.'

The dictionary gives 'went' as 'an obsolete past tense and past participle of *wend*, now used as past tense of *go*. (From Old English *wendan*.)' Try explaining that to a speaker of Glescaranto.

'Whissa pass parciple, Mac? Whissa absolute pass tense?'

A teacher of English in one of our comprehensive schools tried to tell her class that they should say: 'We have gone.' Her pupils told her, commiseratingly: 'At's jist the wey the posh folk talk.' Many pupils who know it is regarded by their teachers as bad grammar may persist in using it rather than sound as if they are deserting their classmates.

Another favourite — and one much used by public orators in No Mean City — is 'fur tae'. This one was used by Robert Burns and that ought to establish it in the favour of Scottish patriots: it occurs also in English dialects, as in 'Old Uncle Tom Cobley' — 'For I want for to go to Widdicombe Fair' — so it may (like 'I have went') have been good grammar at one time. Not that the average Glaswegian is deeply concerned about sticking to Shakespeare or any other 'well of English undefiled'.

There is a story of two Scotswomen visiting London and studying in an art gallery a painting of 'Salome Dancing Before Herod'.

'Whit's it say, Aggie? Ah huvnae goat ma specs oan.'

'It says, "Soalamin dancin in front o' Harrod's".'

'Och, Aggie, he nivver done that — he nivver done that.'

'Ach away, Bessie, he mustuv did it, or he wid nivveruv goat his photey took at it.'

A terrible slander on my highly educated countrywomen, of course, but it illustrates the quite frequent mix-up of 'done' and 'did' in Scots-English. Also 'took' is very often used instead of 'taken'. To even things up, the Scots form 'taen', which means 'taken', is just as often used instead of 'took'.

'Oh hullaw rerr!'

'Ah big yer pardon? I don't think Ah ken you.'

'Here, naw, neither div Ah ken you. Ah've went an' taen ye fur somebody else.'

'Ah must have a double.'

'Please yersel, Mac, as lang as ye can pey for it.'

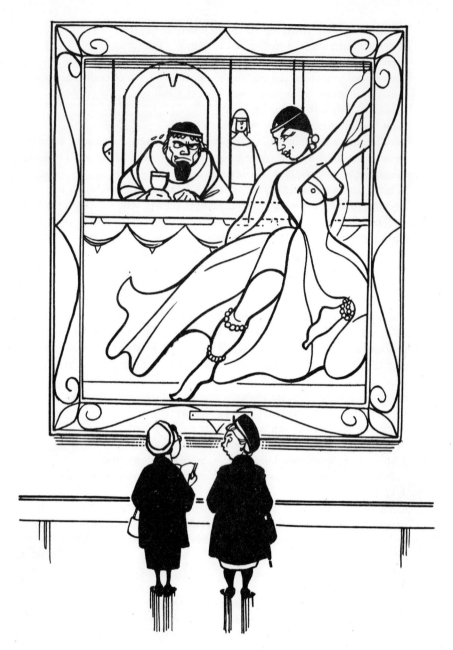

'It says, "Soalamin dancin in front o' Harrod's".'

One hears it every day:

'Can Ah get a bus here that'll tak me tae Paisley?'

'If ye staun there, missiz, ye'll get took tae a morchery.'

Older Scots sometimes say 'tooken':

'Ah shoulda been at the wane's christenin but Ah goat tooken ill.'

The life and soul of the party may be told:

'Here, you're a right coamic. Ye've mistooken yer profession.'

So someone accused of a misdemeanour may plead: 'It wiz jist a case o' mistooken eedentity an' Ah could nivveruv did it, fur Ah wiznae there.'

In Scots we say: 'Ah'll mabe no can get' and 'He widnae could manage'. So don't be surprised if it crops up also in some of our attempts to put on the English, sometimes despised as 'pittin oan the patter' (the *t*s are silent, as usual).

The double negative is used, particularly for emphasis:

'They wid nane o' them hae nane o' it.'

(None of them would have any of it.)

Two women meeting in Argyle Street:

'Oh, hullaw, izzat you?'

'Ay, an' izzat you?'

'Ay. — Here, it's no you.'

'Naw, an' it's no you.'

'Naw, sherr's daith, it's no nane o' us.'

It can express extreme disgust:

'Hoo much did at man gie ye fur helpin him aff the bus wi's bag?'

'Ah niver goat nuchin.'

When the teacher heard one boy say: 'If Ah hudduv kent, Ah wid nivveruv went,' she asked another boy in the class: 'What ought Johnny to have said?' and the bright one replied: 'If Ah hudduv knew.'

'Ken' and 'know' are interchangeable in everyday speech. Glaswegians share with almost every other group of English speakers the irritating habit of punctuating their sentences with 'you know'. But sometimes they do their best to relieve the monotony by substituting 'Ken?'

'Ah wiz staunin at yoan coarner, ken? Foarnenst the poast office, ken? Minin ma ain business, ken? An this fella spoke tae me — nivver seen um in ma life afore, ken? He says, ''Kin ye gie a helpin haun tae a pal at's oan the flerr?'' Chancin his haun, ken? Nivver seen um afore, ken? But ah wiz leery fur um — Ah jist taen wan luk at um an Ah said, ''Soarry, pal, Ah'm oan the flerr masel.'' If ye seen the dirty luck he gien me an aff he stumped roon the coarner. Chancin his haun, ken? He'd huv tae be up gey early tae catch me, but.'

'Whit kinna fella wiz he?'

'Scruff. An Ah seen right away he taen a bucket.'

'Oot fur a reviver, like.'

'Ay, an if he hudduv been a pal, Ah widduv helped um, ken? But Ah haurly hud the price o a hauf fur masel.'

Our Home Guard sergeant used to order us: 'Keep yer eyes in front: ye've saw me afore.'

Many Glaswegians, of all classes, jocularly use the phrase: 'Get fell in, yous!' — supposed to have been uttered in all seriousness by an N.C.O.

If many persist in saying 'Ah've went' because they think it ensures their acceptance in the best working-class circles, many even of those considered well educated say 'between you and I' under the delusion, apparently, that it sounds more refined than 'between you and me'.

One Glasgow teacher made a brave effort to get this right. She asked her star pupil, 'What's wrong with "between you and I"?' and immediately he replied: 'It should be "between you and I and the gatepost".'

Shakespeare used 'you and I' in this ungrammatical way, so the idiom has been in English for over three hundred years. Since 'alright' (for 'all right') has won its way into the *Shorter Oxford Dictionary*, it may be that one of these days 'between you and I' will be accepted by Fowler's *Modern English Usage*.

Most of us prefer to say 'It's me' rather than 'it is I', which we feel is just not us. Just too, too 'weel pitten-oan'.

At the Golden Gates:

'Whawzzat oot err?'

'It is I.'

'Ach, anurra skillteacher!' (Another schoolteacher.)

In Scots we say 'knifes', 'wifes', 'wolfs', rather than 'knives', 'wives' and 'wolves', and this sometimes spills over into our English. I can never bring myself to say 'hooves': to me horses and cuddies (donkeys) will always have hoofs.

Some professional Scots remain proud of Scottish ways of pronouncing English words. A Glasgow Sheriff, who normally spoke Panloaf, once protested to me, as if to convince me of his true Scottishness: 'But I still say "boilt".'

'Grampaw,' asked a wee Glasgow boy, 'wiz you in Noah's Ark?'

'Nut at all,' replied the old man, 'nut at all.'

'Hoo did ye no get droont, well?' asked the puzzled youngster.

One woman discussing her family record of religious observance said: 'Ma man yist tae be a great kirk haun, but noo he's went an' turnt oot a reglar hunkerslider.'

A usually polite husband affronted his wife by belching in the bus queue.

'Menners, Joack,' she rebuked him.

'Whidgie mean, menners?'

'Weel, ye riftit, did ye no?'

'Sure'n Ah did: d'ye no ken the aul sayin, but: Better a tim hoose (an empty house) nor an ill tenant.'

'Saw right fur you. Ye gien me a rid face, but.'

A housewife having home repairs done asked the joiner:

'Are ye sherr yer wid's saizunt?' (Are you sure your timber is seasoned?)

'Lissen, missiz,' he answered indignantly, 'ma timmer aye saizons itsel afore Ah'm feenisht oan the joab.'

'Lang-nebbit' (long-nosed or many-syllabled) words and Latin or Greek technicalities, especially medical terms, are inevitably mangled. Bronchitis used to be known in Glasgow as 'the broonkaidies', but now it is 'ra bronnickles':

'Ay, ma man is awfae bawthert wirra assma, but Ah'd be fine masel if it wiznae furra bronnickles.'

The disease we hear most about is 'athuritis', and quite a number of Glaswegians complain of 'ulsters'.

'If Ah mak up ma mine tae visit ma sister in Australia,' said one aul wife, 'the wan thing Ah kin haurly face is the thocht o getting knuckle-latit agane aw thae toapical diseases.'

When the doctor asked the old lady in hospital if the nurse had taken her temperature, she answered:

'Naw, naebody taen ma tempitcher. The only thing that lassie taen wiz ma black grapes.'

Old Scots with an intolerance of 'lang-nebbit', and especially of new words, will often tell the younger generation: 'Speak Scoatch or whussle!' but in fact Scots has a lot of 'lang-nebbit' words of its own and many of them still thrive in modern Glasgow:

'Thur nae needcessitie fur aw thae whigmaleeries.'

'Ah dinnae ken whit she fancies she is, walkin up the street that wiggeltie waggeltie wey.'

'Ay, an' her man's a rale shauchmatram (dilapidated person) wi a kinna shirpit (withered) leg — aye walks shilliefittit (dragging his feet), ken?'

'That wife's goat a gift fur stertin a sterrheid stishie (starting an uproar on the stairhead or tenement landing)'.

'Ma man's the awfayest beggar tae sweer, but he says he jist yaizes that kinna words tae mak the sentences clink.'

'Fancies his-sel as a singer wi his barratone voice — but yoan's a hurly-barra that's needin some ile.' (A wheelbarrow that needs some oil.)

'She gets ferr kerrit awaw wi thae shoogieshoo dances at the diskateck, but he jist wauchles alang nivver keepin step.'

'Ay, Ah dinnae ken whit she sees in um — he's a shachly wee bachle at the best o' times.'

'Bachles' are dilapidated footwear and the word is often applied to a person who is in the same sort of condition. 'Shachly' means shuffling, and 'shachly wee bachle' is probably the best-known of Glasgow expressions outside of 'peely-wally'.

Wee Georgie Wood, in his dressing-room at the Glasgow Empire when there was still such a theatre, told me that as a boy he had gone to school for a brief spell in Saltcoats: 'They called me a wee peely-wally!'

'China? Me no China, me Poland.'

Back to that legendary Glasgow classroom. This time the teacher was puzzled by Johnny's answer to her question: 'What do we get from foreign lands?'

Without hesitation, and with finality, he replied: 'Biscuits.'

'Come, come, now, surely that isn't all you get from foreign lands.'

'Please, miss, Ah thought ye said, ''Macfaurlane Lang's''.'

Macfarlane Lang & Co. Ltd. (biscuit manufacturers) was on the tongues of Glaswegians in the Twenties and Thirties also for another reason. Those were the days of rhyming slang, some of which is still mixed into the local dialect, and 'Macfaurlane Lang' (or simply 'The Macfaurlane') became rhyming slang for 'rhyming slang'.

'Aw the hooks, crooks and coamic singers is talkin the Macfaurlane,' I used to hear. Tommy Lorne, the squeaky-voiced Glasgow comic who dominated music-hall and pantomime between the wars, called it 'the fly talk', and would exclaim to some feed who used it on the stage: 'Oh, the fly talk? Are you a fly man?' Nowadays 'fly men' are 'spivs', if they have not graduated to 'hard men'.

Rhyming slang is not exclusive to Glasgow, by any means. It is popular among Cockneys, who refer to the bottle as 'Aristotle'. Australians also are notably prone to it. But Glasgow's 'Macfaurlane' has its peculiarities and also its favourites from the world currency of the language.

Probably the commonest 'Macfaurlane' word in the city is 'china', for 'mate' (from the rhyming slang, 'china plate'). In the last war a typical kindly Glaswegian strode into a pub determined to stand his hand to some representative of our Allied Forces. He picked on one foreign-looking lad in battledress and hailed him with: 'Hullaw, china! Whit ur ye huvvin?'

The soldier looked puzzled, then pointed at his shoulder-flash: 'China? Me no China, me Poland.'

Nothing dates so quickly as slang, but many Glasgow men still talk of going up to Sauchiehall Street to 'meet the chinas'.

In the days of the Billy Boys, the Nunny Boys, the Norman Conks and other Glasgow gangs, the members of these organisations were usually known to one another as 'ra boys', often used ecstatically in the phrase 'raboysaboys'. Rhyming slang for 'boys' is 'San Toys', and many a lesser Glasgow gang adopted the name 'San Toy' preceded by the name of the district which it decorated with its swagger.

A weapon much in favour in those days among the toughs was the razor, soon nicknamed 'House of Fraser'.

Famous Glasgow names have been used in the creation of this fly lingo, which circulates among the sporting fraternity as well as among 'hooks and crooks'. If you are told to 'Get aff yer Elky', it is not as rude as it sounds. There was a great wee Glasgow boxer called Elky Clark, who lost an eye in a title fight in New York with Fidel la Barba and who later became a newspaper colleague of mine. His name was used as rhyming slang for 'mark', so 'Get aff yer Elky!' meant 'Get aff yer mark!'

As a 'mark' in crooks' language might mean an intended victim or a time fixed for an illegal operation, 'Elky' has been used in these senses also.

Similarly 'Benny Lynch' came to mean 'a cinch' among gamblers. It was appropriate in the days when Benny, flyweight champion of the world and a Gorbals boy, was winning all his fights.

People who use rhyming slang are not always conscious of its origin. They pick it up from their 'chinas' and use it because they think it sounds smart. Many Glaswegians, for instance, say: 'Nut oan yer Nelly' without knowing what 'Nelly' really means. The expression has become part of everyday speech and it sounds very Glasgow, but it may well have come from America or London. 'Nelly' is 'Nelly Duff', rhyming slang for 'natural puff' or the breath of life, and the phrase means 'Not so long as you are breathing' or 'Not on your life!'

Comics have used it a lot on the Glasgow stage and it always gets one of those 'deep calls to dirty deep' laughs as if it meant a whole lot more than it really does. Perhaps part of the attraction of these vulgarisms is their vagueness and their suggestion of what the aul wife calls 'double intenders.'

Slang is used not only to confuse strangers but to establish the user as one of 'yous'. And there are other varieties besides rhyming tags. Every schoolboy in his day tries his hand at talking in back slang, reversing whole words. The one which has stayed in the dialect is 'slop' for a policeman. It is 'polis' spelt backwards and telescoped slightly.

Some slang is really quite ancient. For instance, recently I heard a young fly man refer to the train as 'the rattler'. He would be surprised to hear that this was the word used by his great-great-grandfather for the stage-coach.

But Glasgow speech is often inventive and new words are born overnight. There is the spoonerism 'champ dancer' for 'chancer'. It was born in the Dennistoun Palais de Danse in the days of the big bands, when a girl complained: 'He tellt me he wiz a champ dancer but Ah fan oot he wiz a damp chancer.' It is a handy phrase for warning a friend that he is being 'conned'.

Street traders, 'mumpers' (beggars) and travelling folk originated a lot of the slang which percolates into the speech of people far removed from their way of life. At 'ra barras' one hears snatches of Yiddish such as 'finnif' for five, and the multilingual jargon of the 'grafter' (kerb salesman) 'fannying the hedge' (gathering a crowd).

Long before 'gezump' came into use to describe reneging on a house sale agreement, I heard it employed to describe rubbish sold round the doors under brand names chosen to look or sound like those of established firms. A fly acquaintance told me: 'Noo that Ah'm oan the rubber sole (the Dole) Ah get the oadd joab sellin gezump roon the hooses, or sometimes it's jist keepin a butcher's (butcher's hook — look or lookout) fur the bizzies (busybodies or plain-clothes police) fur some china daein (robbing) some place.'

Another of his casual jobs, he told me, was looking out for 'wally dugs' (mugs) who could be 'taken' by confidence tricksters.

Bingo has put a number of slang words into recent circulation. An old and much respected Anglican clergyman surprised me when, on my congratulating him on his healthy appearance, he replied: 'I'm clickety-click,' meaning he was sixty-six. But now even the bingo-callers have grown tired of such slang as 'dinky doo' for twenty-two and 'Kelly's eye' for one. Now it is 'all the twos' and 'one alone'.

Another effect of slang is to make petty larceny and other run-of-the-mill crime sound almost genteel. For instance, 'half-inch' (rhyming slang for 'pinch') never sounds so bad as 'steal', and it is frequently used for 'stealing by finding' on the principle — 'Finds keeps, loasses greets (loser cries)'. Many an object lying around on a shop floor or in a shipyard has been 'half-inched' by characters who would be deeply offended if ever accused of stealing.

Although some modern slang has come to Glasgow from America through the influence of the media, from American comic papers to TV shows, some of it is really Scots come home in slightly mutilated form and often with its meaning subtly changed. For instance, in Scotland many of us now say 'jiggery-pokery' instead of the good old Scots form 'jookery-pawkery' (from 'jook' meaning to dodge and 'pawky' meaning sly).

Similarly 'skulduggery' has come into currency with the meaning of using the brain (skull) in conspiracy to defraud or 'with intent to deceive'. It is an American corruption of Robert Burns's word 'sculduddery', which had quite a different meaning — 'bawdy', otherwise pornography.

It is not generally appreciated that Robert Burns introduced a lot of the slang of his day into his poems along with genuine local dialect. In this he followed the lead of his Edinburgh predecessor, Robert Fergusson. It was the practice of other poets — notably Francois Villon in medieval France and the half-Scottish Lord Byron shortly after Burns's day.

Robert Fergusson used 'dossied doun' for 'lay down to sleep' and modern Glaswegians use 'loabby-doassers' for people who sleep in the lobbies or landings of tenements. Model lodging houses, or 'working men's hotels', are commonly referred to as 'doass-hooses'.

Fergusson refers to 'my hindmost rook' for 'my last penny'. Glaswegians still say 'Ah wiz rooksed', meaning 'skint'. But many of Fergusson's slang terms are obsolete now, such as 'macaronis' for fops or dandies, 'coulis' for servants or porters, 'joot' for liquor (usually third-rate or almost lethal), 'benders' (elbow-benders) for boozers and 'gez' or 'gezy' for wig.

Gaelic figures little in Glasgow slang, though in its tinker's Shelta form (in which the words are twisted almost in a back slang) it has given one word to the travelling folk and others — 'toby'. This comes from Irish Gaelic 'bothar', a road, twisted into 'tobar'. Now it is rhyming-slanged as 'George Robey', but tramping 'the high toby' has become a thing of the past, except for hitch-hikers who mostly have little intention of doing any real walking.

Glasgow folk quickly adopt modern slang, such as 'chopper' for helicopter, or 'jogger' for the brave people running round the city in track suits or flimsier garments. Two of these characters were jogging round Bellahouston Park and two lazier types were looking on quizzically.

'Izzat a cuppla athaletes?'

'Naw, it's joggers. They're daein it tae keep their beer bellies doon.'

'Ah think they're nuts.'

'At's right. Joggernuts.'

So a new slang term comes into the Glescaranto vocabulary.

Romany and Didikai (non-Romany gypsies) have contributed odd phrases such as 'Ay, ye're a shan gadgie' (a fine fellow, used sarcastically) and 'A kushti gry' for a good horse. These are heard only in show circles and in the Borders where the Falls or Faas reigned as gypsy royalty. But 'Ah'll mar ye' (I'll murder you), 'stir' for jail and 'bevvy' for a booze-up seem to be of gypsy origin and ultimately from Sanskrit (the Romanies came from India, not Egypt as the Scots believed).

One word survives from 'Parliaree', the fake Italian of the show folk. It is 'nanty' (*niente*) for 'nothing'. I have heard a Glasgow woman tell her small boy, 'If ye dinnae stoap mumpin, ye'll get nanty.' (If you do not stop begging you will get nothing.)

'Parliaree' circulated in the world of theatrical digs and landladies picked it up. 'Nanty munjarlee' meant nothing to eat; 'Nanty dinarlee', no money; 'Nanty letty', nowhere to sleep. I have heard comics use these expressions to one another in the variety theatres, but this kind of showbiz 'Tally' (Italian) is commoner among circus folk.

Indian Boy Scouts with turbines on their heads.

Our Glasgow Press — now sadly depleted — played a great part in keeping many of the city's expressions in circulation. Newspaper writers, both native and 'in-comers', have always been sensitive to the phrases which they came across in their intimate contact with the public.

As in much of our work we were mingling with the more racy elements in the community, and hearing their 'picturesque speech and patter', as the *Reader's Digest* calls it, we naturally became repositories for a good deal of Glasgow speech. And inevitably, when we had the opportunity, we employed typical city expressions in our 'Talk of the. Town', 'City and Clyde', 'Clydeside Echoes' and other popular columns.

Just before my time the big name in the *Glasgow Evening News* was that of Neil Munro. Although he is now most famous as Hugh Foulis, the author of *Para Handy*, and regarded as a Highland rather than a Lowland Scots writer, he was as expert in the Glasgow dialect as in that of the Highland skipper of the Clyde 'puffer' (coastal steamer). He wrote a series of sketches about a Glasgow waiter called 'Erchie' with 'a flet fit an' a warm hert'.

When I started on that paper in 1928 its literary stars were Robins Millar and Norman Bruce. Robins, though born and reared in British Guiana as a missionary's son, wrote Glasgow dialect stories about 'The Redoubtable Bella' who worked at 'the biscuits' and who referred frequently to her uncle from 'Murrawell' (Motherwell).

Norman Bruce was one of a succession of writers who churned out the daily joke column, 'Clydeside Echoes', and he invented a series on the Erskine Ferry, 'all sailing by pure chain', which was a parody of *Para*

Handy and a satire on the ferry at Erskine, which did in fact work by haulage on a chain. Erskine now has a famous bridge.

The first day I reported for work at the *News* I was put alongside Cecil Orr, a cartoonist for the paper, and he and I pored over the morning papers looking for news items which we could work into gags for 'Clydeside Echoes'. Cecil was an amateur entertainer in musicals who later wrote and illustrated a book in collaboration with Lupino Lane, entitled *How to Be a Comedian*, and there was a colourful legend about how he had got his job on the paper.

David R. Anderson, our editor-in-chief on what was then part of the Rothermere Empire, was artistic, and when he was appointed, Lord Rothermere sent a telegram to the manager: 'Tell Anderson to get his hair cut!' When Cecil came to him for a start as a cartoonist, so the story goes, he mentioned his stage work, and Anderson asked: 'Can you do a back flip?' (a back somersault). Cecil flipped — and got the job.

There was still a *Weekly Record* then, as well as the *Daily Record* and the *Sunday Mail*, and the editor of the weekly, who was later my editor on the evening paper, was John Conn, who is fondly remembered for a monumental remark.

It happened in the Glasgow Arts Club, of which David R. Anderson was a flamboyant member. Anderson asked Conn along to the club to introduce him to some of its very artistic members in the hope that he might lift the very journalistic Conn out of his popular-paper groove.

Anderson installed himself in the centre of the distinguished company with his back to the mantelpiece. Conn enjoyed the comfort of a deep armchair. While Anderson and his friends were discussing art and 'making like Benedetto Croce', Conn dropped off to sleep, to be awakened by his editor-in-chief trying to bring him into the conversation.

'What do *you* think of art, Conn?' asked Anderson.

Conn replied drowsily: 'I think it's a bugger.'

Such phrases, in a city such as Glasgow, become immortal. No one enjoyed telling the story more than the two characters in the dialogue, each from his own distinct angle.

Behind it was a struggle between an 'arty-farty' editor-in-chief who wanted to elevate his papers and their readers, and a man who had begun his newspaper career in the Isle of Man, taking in the money for circulation and advertisements as well as writing for his paper.

Glasgow then had the grand old *Evening Citizen*, the *Bulletin* and other 'late lamented' publications as well as the *Evening Times*, the *Glasgow Herald*, the *Daily Record* and the *Sunday Mail* which still survive and carry on the tradition of holding a mirror (and often a highly comical one) up to city life. The *Sunday Post* also fortunately survives with its Glasgow premises as well as its Dundee home base. Its cartoon features, 'Oor Wullie' and 'The Broons', chime in with the Clydeside humour even if they stem from the countryside and smaller towns of Angus.

What characters there were on the staffs of the Glasgow papers in those days! In the *News*, and later in the Glasgow office of *The Scottish Daily Express*, we had John S. Clarke. He had been a circus clown and a lion-tamer, and in his lunch-hour he would drop into Wilson's Zoo in Argyle Street (under the Heelanman's Umbrella or railway bridge), and later in Oswald Street, to exercise a pair of lionesses. As a Glasgow colleague described it to me:

'Ye widnae believe it but Ah'm tellin ye: Joahn went in this wee cage wi thae twa lions — lassie lions, ken? — an' the first thing he done wiz picked up a whup and cracked it an' they ran roon an' roon, an' ye'll no believe this but Ah'm tellin ye, the nixt thing he diz is fling the bliddy whup awa on the flerr — an' wan o' thae lions picks it up an' brings it owre tae um — jist like a dug!'

When John was M.P. for Maryhill he alarmed his brother-legislators by taking snakes into the House of Commons. He was told not to do that again, but he remarked drily, 'They weren't the first snakes there — nor would they be the last.'

He was a collector of antiques as well as a keen zoologist and had been stopped on another occasion by the master-at-arms at Westminster and shown how to hang up his sword in the cloakroom as weapons were forbidden in the House. John had a great sense of mischief and I have no doubt that this prompted his attempt to swing a claymore or a broadsword in the Mother of Parliaments.

One of John's admirers, a young journalist called Eddie Campbell, learned to perform with the lions in the cage, and started studying German in order to talk to circus lions, which usually have German trainers and respond to commands in that language.

For a while John S. Clarke shared an office room in the *Daily Record* building at 67 Hope Street with another amazing character, John James Miller.

John James was a member of a highly educated family from Alva in Central Scotland. One of his brothers was the minister of Milnathort and another was headmaster of a high school. But John had preferred the country life and had worked as a quarry-man and performed as a Highland athlete, particularly as a wrestler.

In the days long before 'all-in', he had figured in more than one fatal wrestling bout.

John S. and John James were uneasy room-mates. John James objected to the specimens which people sent in after reading John S.'s articles on animal life.

'There wiz yae deid rat,' John James told me, 'cam rowed up in a broon paper parcel, an' Joahn S. wiz awa oan some trip, an' av coorse Ah nivver interfered wi onything o' his, an' Ah didnae ken whit it wiz till it stertit stinkin. But b'Goad Ah shin goat redd o't efter that.'

John S. was lean and bald, with a Bob Hope nose and a keen face. When he came into the office with a chimpanzee on his shoulder, John Conn asked him: 'Is this your son looking for a job on the paper?'

John James was hefty, with black hair and a Joe Stalin moustache. He wrote wrestling articles and used technical expressions. Once I was foolish enough to ask him what a 'hipe' was, and he showed me and I landed in a heap in a corner. I never asked him again what anything was.

He used to boast: 'Ah'm the only man that ivver stepped aff a cairt intae a joab on a paper.'

How it happened was this. While he worked as a quarryman and went round the games as an athlete, he sent reports in to the *Record* of these sporting events. One evening he realised he could not get the report in on time if he relied on train or bus. So, in his own words, 'Ah druv intae Glesca in the cairt, an' tied the hoarse up in Cadogan Street.'

He wanted to hand his report personally to John Conn.

'Conn wiznae in. They tellt me he wiz ower at the Corn Exchange at some perty tae yin o' the lads they were seein aff.'

I was the one who was being seen off, as I had just settled for a job in Jamaica. As it happened I had been deputising on the *Record* for a book-maker called John S. Barron, who wrote the boxing reports and had taken ill. My departure for Jamaica left a vacancy for a boxing reporter and John James got it 'the nicht he stepped aff the cairt' — in fact, his appointment was settled in the Corn Exchange in the midst of my send-off party. He was well installed in Hope Street by the time I got back to Glasgow.

John James wrote by choice in a mixture of Scots and English — a bucolic style which Norman Bruce parodied in 'Clydeside Echoes'. 'Airtin' yont the bit' (walking up the road), 'aiblins' (perhaps) and 'oxters' (armpits) were a few of the big man's favourite expressions, and Norman Bruce would begin his parodies with 'Airtin yont the bit wi' my aiblins ablow my oxters...' John James curled his Joe Stalin moustache in contempt.

Another of our characters was a reporter who committed howlers. 'The most colourful participants in the Jamboree were the Indian Boy Scouts with turbines on their heads' was one of his masterpieces.

Once he had not covered a show at the Empire so he 'lifted' the report

'Is this your son looking for a job on the paper?'

from the *Glasgow Herald* and re-wrote it for the evening paper. The *Herald* said a certain comic 'excelled in light raillery' and our reporter changed it to 'The hit of the evening was the light railway act'. Later he was challenged about this but stuck to his guns, describing a fantastic act in which a man had gone round the gallery on a light railway and on a monocycle.

Every newspaper has had a reporter like that in its day.

The *Record* had a great comic column, 'Bats in the Belfry' by 'The Gangrel' (Harold S. Stewart), who wrote good Glasgow dialect, including a poem about a favourite city custom, 'Leanin' oot the windae wi' ma elbaes in ma hauns.' He wrote scripts for 'Bees in the Bonnet' on the BBC — another institution which has done much to project the Glasgow image and the dialect.

'It diznae suit a beggar tae be berrfaced.'

Between the wars, when I was working on the *Glasgow Evening News* with John Conn, a frequent visitor to our editorial offices was the Clincher, selling a newspaper with the same title as his *nom-de-guerre*.

We always took a copy at a cost of sixpence at least. In those days sixpence had much more than the value of the 2½p which is supposed to be its present-day equivalent. As the newspaper which he sold us each time was exactly the same as before — an edition he had had printed in the remote past — he was doing quite well.

Although there are still buskers 'giein it laldy' (belting it out) in Buchanan Street and around Exchange Square, there is no one nowadays quite so picturesque as the Clincher. He had a snow-white beard and moustache like a big-store Santa Claus and he wore a frock coat and a top hat.

At Christmas time he walked up Buchanan Street or along Gordon Street or Sauchiehall Street with a placard on his back: 'Kiss me under the mistletoe!' At the bottom of the placard, and just above the tail of his frock coat, hung the Yuletide mistletoe sprig. Like all of the Clincher's jokes, it was a hardy annual.

His newspaper had originally been printed in the first Labour Premiership of James Ramsay MacDonald, whom he nicknamed 'The Lossie Drifter', after the fishing vessels which worked from the statesman's native

Lossiemouth. The Clincher's paragraph remained in the paper no matter whose Government was in power or office and it read: 'The Rt. Hon. James Ramsay MacDonald is the son of an Irish tattie-howker (potato-lifter). As a Prime Minister he is a good tattie-howker wasted.'

That was a sample of the mordant humour of this old character with the kindly, beaming, Santa Claus face and the gentle Glasgow voice. At his stance in Buchanan Street, with his papers in his hand, he attracted the attention of passers-by with the chanted, charitable message:

'Awa hame (away home) an' gie yer Granny a moothfae (mouthful) o whisky!'

Surnamed Petrie, the Clincher had at one time been a barber somewhere around the Sautmarket, but he had always been of a political, polemical, argumentative disposition, favouring the Radical cause.

In his barber shop he argued politics with his customers. One customer took exception to the Clincher's views, and made the mistake of voicing his opposition while the barber was standing over him, razor in hand.

'Anither word oot o you,' said the Clincher, 'an' Ah'll gie ye a rid grauvit!' A 'rid grauvit' in Glasgow is a red scarf, but it is the toughs' way of describing 'a sliced wizzen' or cut throat.

On the Glasgow principle of 'Ah'll gie ye a slap on the jaw an' there it's!' — Petrie drew the back of his razor over the man's Adam's apple and the customer clasped his throat and ran out into the street sreaming that he was being murdered by this modern Sweeny Todd.

Glasgow's police — a more alert bunch, perhaps, than their Strathclyde successors — were immediately on the scene and Petrie was taken into custody and hauled before a bailie in the city court. The bailie was so flabbergasted at this conduct in a barber shop that he ordered the Clincher to be taken to Gartnavel for a mental examination.

They did not keep him long in there. He was probably more of a handful than the usual run of people who 'needit their heids luckt'. Whatever happened, he was shortly discharged with a certificate saying that he was quite sane.

This was a great triumph for the Clincher, who thereafter went around with the certificate in his pocket. In his political oratory, usually at shipyard or works gates, he used to wave the paper in the air and say: 'Ah'm the only man here that can prove he's no a heid case.'

Another of his phrases to lunch-time listeners was: 'Ay, ye aw think Ah'm daft, but jist wait till that horn blaws an' we'll see wha's daft.'

If ever the Clincher's political oratory had been serious, latterly it had become just a form of entertainment, and a way of 'makkin an oanist maik or twa' (making an honest halfpenny or two).

In this he was following an old Glasgow tradition of the street orator, like the one who used to wag his wooden leg and bring it down with a bump proclaiming, 'Ah'm here fur tae mak a stump speech.'

The greatest of the street orators had been Hawkie, the favourite of the literary men. of the city last century. Hawkie's real name was William Cameron. He had tried his hand without success at several types of employment, including that of a dominie (schoolmaster), but had ended up on the streets of Glasgow, an unrepentant drunkard and a most original city wit.

It was Hawkie who said, on being told to go and have a shave: 'It diznae suit a beggar tae be berrfaced', but barefaced he was to the end, as the Clincher was despite his ample white beard.

Hawkie had what the Glaswegians called 'a shirpit (withered) leg' and he walked around on a crutch with the additional aid of a stick which he waved in his Argyle Street and Trongate oratory.

He seems to have been a master of epigram and figure of speech, such as 'That maks twa o us, as the coo said tae the cuddie' (That makes two of us as the cow said to the donkey) and (when asked what he had done with an unrepaid loan), 'It's awa whaur the coo calved the cuddie' (It's away where the cow gave birth to the donkey). Cows and donkeys seem to have occurred a lot in his imagery.

Proverbial wit is to a great extent preserved by Glasgow orators, whether their platform is wooden or 'caussay stanes' (the granite setts of the old causeways or carriageways). My favourite from their lore also concerns a cow: 'Awbody tae their ain taste, as the aul wife said whun she kissed the coo.' (Everybody to their own taste, as the old woman said when she kissed the cow.)

Here are a few of the proverbs one still hears in Glasgow, passed on from grandparents to children and thus assured of at least another generation's life-span:

'A gaun fit's aye gettin though it's only a staved tae.'

(A walking foot is always gaining something though it may be only a stubbed toe.)

'Mony a bride breks her elbae on the kirk lintel.'

(Many a bride breaks her elbow on the side of the church door — that is to say, if she showed a disposition to do housework before her marriage, her enthusiasm declines once she has got her man.)

'Shoemakers' wanes iz aye warst shoad.'

(Shoemakers'·children are always worst shod.)

'A herry man's a wealthy man: a herry wife's a witch.'

('herry' is the Glasgow way of saying 'hairy', as in 'Herry Merry (Hairy

Mary) an' ra Hardman', a popular local folksong.)

'There mony a lee tellt at the neb o a pen.'

(There is many a lie told at the tip of a pen.)

'Ma son's ma son urrie gets um a wife: ma dochter's ma dochter awra days o her life.'

(My son's my son till he gets him a wife: my daughter's my daughter all the days of her life.)

Despite the attempted anglicisation of the schools, which seems to me to have largely the effect of producing the crudest 'Scots English', some good old expressions die hard. Here are some:

'Wan man's meat's anither man's poozhin', 'Ah'm as dry's a rid herrin', 'He's coarn beef (rhyming slang) — Ah mean he's as deef's a doornail', 'Ah seen um takkin the braid urra road — as foo's a puggie' (I saw him taking the breadth of the road — as drunk as a monkey), ''Chynges are lichtsome,'' as the aul wife said whun her man dee'd' ('Changes are easy to take,' as the old woman said when her husband died), 'The clartier the cosier' (The dirtier the dwelling place the cosier it is — a saying often used to comfort folk compelled to dwell in overcrowded conditions, on the argument that all those coal fires in an old Glasgow tenement ensured at least heat for the inhabitants.)

When someone is criticised for bad conduct, the complainer will often be asked, 'Whit kin ye expeck fae a soo but a grumph?' (What can you expect from a sow but a grunt?)

The impatient trainee is told: 'Laddie, ye hae tae creep afore ye gang.' (You must creep before you walk.)

Of too conservative or socially timid people it is said: 'They're feart fur the day they nivver saw.' (They are afraid of a day they never saw.)

''Hunger's gidd kitchen,'' as the aul wife said whun she ett ur bits.' ('Hunger is good seasoning for any food,' as the old woman said when she ate her boots — as Chaplin did in *The Gold Rush*. Actually 'Kitchen' means some tasty bit added to a meal, such as fried bread or a piece of bacon.)

'That's the ticket fur tottie-soup.' (That's the very thing — the ticket for potato-soup, a survival from cattle shows or perhaps from city soup-kitchens in days of distress.)

A modern beggar of the hippie variety was asked, 'Why can't you be respectable like your old father? He looked like an elder.'

'Izzat so? Well, Ah feel like a Younger.' (A reference to a well-known brand of ale.)

Hawkie once waylaid a gentleman in Argyle Street with: 'Byde a blink (wait a moment) till Ah tell ye something.'

He was told: 'You'll get nothing from me: you're drunk.'

'Ay, mebbe,' he replied, 'but Ah'm no hauf sae drunk as Ah'd like tae be.'

A shrewd Glaswegian said recently: 'Dinnae gie thae beggars a wing or a maik (a penny or a halfpenny). They're making siller like sclatestanes.' (They're making money like slates.)

But a heckler who threatened to 'queer the pitch' for one of our street orators was told by the 'gabberlunyie man': 'Awa ye go — ye huvnae the brains fur a beggar!'

Skilful begging is described as 'layin oan the cadge'. Of a late lamented master of the craft a brother-mendicant said, 'Ay, he couldnae hauf lay oan the cadge, but some o thae yins noo ken as muckle aboot it as grumphie kens aboot grammar.' (As much as a pig knows of grammar.)

'Ah dinnae aye see I.C.I. tae eye wi you.'

Queen Mary, the sometimes severe-looking consort of King George V, and the rather tragic figure in the Abdication drama of her son, Edward VIII, relaxed in the company of Glasgow's first Socialist Lord Provost, Sir John Stewart.

Enjoying the Scots hospitality of the Lord Provost's Room (which, unlike the Corporation dining-room, was not 'dry'), she chatted amiably with the old brush-manufacturer and plied him with questions about social conditions in the city.

'I may say,' she remarked, 'I have noticed an improvement in the apparent health of the Glasgow children.'

'Ay, ma'am,' agreed Sir John, 'they're no sae peely-wally.'

With a laugh, Her Majesty asked, 'What's peely-wally?' and a bewildered Sir John exclaimed afterwards, 'What could Ah tell ur?'

It was history repeating itself, for Queen Victoria had had a similar difficulty in understanding what were the ingredients of Scotch broth.

'There's tatties intill't an' leeks intill't.'

'What's intill't?'

'There's mebbe carrots intill't an' neeps intill't.'

'Yes, but the thing that puzzles me is what's intill't.'

'Weel, ye see, mem, there aw thae things an' mair intill't.'

Did she ever get the final explanation that 'intill't' means simply 'in it'?

'There aw thae things an' mair intill't.'

Sir John must have found the great 'peely-wally' question an even harder nut to crack, for this favourite Glasgow word means so much more than just 'sickly, not thriving, in obvious need of plenty of good food and fresh air'. To a Glaswegian it described perfectly the condition of the children of the slum and overcrowding period, when 'hurklin banes' (rickets) and 'the decline' (TB) were all too common, and going off in the fever wagon was regarded as almost as final as going off in the hearse.

Children playing in the back courts were told: 'Ye'll get the smit,' which meant infection, often with a fatal disease.

Sir John and his contemporaries, who were in full sway on Glasgow Corporation in my feature-writing days on the *News*, often found Scots their natural medium, and hard to translate.

The new Regional and District, two-tier local government system is beginning to develop comedy of its own, but I doubt if it will ever replace what we often considered the 'pantymine' (or, as we often contracted it, the 'pant') of the old Glasgow Corporation. I succeeded George Blake, the novelist of the shipyards, as 'George Square' — the *nom-de-plume* on a weekly series of humorous articles on the Corporation meetings which were never difficult to make funny. Those old 'Toon Cooncillors' and 'Bylies' played into our hands.

'Yince a bylie aye a bylie' (Once a bailie always a bailie) was the prevalent saying about the magistrates, meaning they would still be given their title by the respectful populace long after they had served their term of office.

'Civic dignitaries' we called them in the Press, in our search for 'elegant variation', but there have been jokes about 'bylies' down the ages, and one of Sir Walter Scott's richest characters is Bailie Nicol Jarvie, a Glasgow magistrate, in *Rob Roy*.

There are still a few Nicol Jarvies knocking about Glasgow, with their dignified mien giving an extra dimension to their often unconscious humour.

There was the one at the banquet who was offered more champagne, and responded: 'Naw, bring iz a dram! Ah cannae be daein wi thae irritatit watters.'

A drunk brought up to the burgh court was asked by the magistrate: 'Noo whit huv ye tae say fur yersel?'

'Ah wiz sittin oapposite ye at the Burns Supper, wiznah? — an' Ah wiznae oany drunker nor yersel, Bylie.'

'Then ye must huv been gey bad. Seeven an' six or five days. Nixt?'

The wife of one old-timer said: 'Ah wiz aye worried that ma man wid faw in the Molendinar burn oan his wey hame fae thae Coarporation banquets, but noo that he's a bylie the poalis aye brings him hame.'

Some of the sayings of 'civic dignitaries' are legendary: 'Sae it's kerrit unamous (carried unanimously) by a great majority that we should gang intae this by degrees gradually.'

Two old hands were growing tired of one of the liberated women of today who had found her way on to the Corporation and was making the most of it.

'Whit wey diz that wumman aye huv tae speak sae much?'

'Dae ye no ken she's loast aw her teeth and her tongue wearies for company?'

Talkative opponents are usually soon categorised as 'nyaffs'. This is another of the favourite Glasgow expressions and its users don't realise that it is medieval in origin. It is 'knaves' in its Scottish form, and 'knaves' were servants in the feudal system, almost 'the lowest form of animal life'.

A hundred years ago a 'wee nyaff' was called a 'nyaffet', and 'nyaffin' was the way these people talked, incessantly. 'He jist kep oan nyaffin awa there till Ah ferr loast ma puggie at um an' couldae cloored um if Ah'd haen an ex handy.' (He just kept on talk-talking away there until I fairly lost my temper at him and could have split his head open if I had had an axe handy.)

A lost of 'nyaffin' or 'nebbin' was done at the Corporation meetings in my day:

'Ma Loard Proavost, whit wey is this no a C paragraph?' (A C paragraph in the printed minutes would be discussed in full Council.)

Sometimes there was some high-class repartee. The instance I cherish in memory was a clash between Victor Warren, an explosives agent and a Progressive (anti-Socialist) member, and Sandy Munro, a Labour worthy, who happened to be 'skelly' (cross-eyed).

Warren, later Lord Provost Sir Victor, snapped at Sandy, who was 'nyaffin' at him: 'Of course, I don't always see eye to eye with you,' an obvious reference to Sandy's affliction, as well as to his Socialistic ideas.

'Naw,' retorted Sandy, quick as a flash, 'an' Ah dinnae aye see I.C.I. tae eye wi you.'

Warren had 'Explosives, Glasgow' as his telegraphic address, and numbered Imperial Chemical Industries among his profitable connections.

A favourite way of expressing dissatisfaction over an official explanation was 'Ay, it's a fine hamahaddie!' an oblique reference to some long-ago grocer's confusion of hams with smoked haddocks.

'Whit is this sum tae dae wi?' the City Treasurer was asked.

'That's the expenses of securing the Act that wiz loast.'

The proposal to do something for posterity awoke one protester from his repose in a part of the Council Chamber known as the 'Boax Bed' or 'Hole-i-the-Waw'.

'Ma Loard Proavist, it's high time fur tae ask oorsels: whit hiz posterity ivver done fur us?'

Glasgow legislators have been noted for their own pronunciations of official jargon. A committee is often a 'coami*tee*', with the accent on the last syllable, but many parts of Scotland accentuate words differently from Standard English: 'adver*ty*zement', 'arith*me*tic', 'coampen*sate*', 'fur*waurd*' (to forward), 'in-*fam*ous', 'la*boarr*itory', 'la*ment*able', 'lu*nat*ic', 'mat*tress*', 'mis*chiev*ious', (an extra 'i' thrown in for good measure), '*poalis*' (police), 'swa*ree*' (soiree), 'the*ay*ter'.

'Ah think yiz huv made a grievious mistake,' said one legislator in the course of a 'noration'. 'An' we dinnae want fur tae be kent fur tae be takkin up a skinnyflint attitude tae a legitmit demand. That hiz nivver been the carriter o "No Mean City".'

Ah, 'No Mean City'! How often has this phrase been used in Glasgow oratory! St Paul's claim to be 'a citizen of no mean city' has been reiterated by many who thought the original author of the phrase was probably Rabbie Burns, and the meaning of the phrase has been variously understood by its users. It was because the phrase was so often employed by our local Ciceros that it was used as the title of a famous novel.

Political oratory has always been a source of entertainment to Glaswegians, and the inspiration of hecklers, especially in Glasgow Green.

One speaker there in the last war was clamouring for a Second Front. 'Ay,' shouted the man at the back of the crowd, 'an' you'd be the first back.'

Sir Robert Bontine Cunninghame-Graham, an aristocratic Socialist, happened to be a descendant of Graham of Claverhouse, known as 'Bonnie Dundee' but also as 'Bliddy Clavers' because he harried the Covenanters. 'Clavers' won the Battle of Killiecrankie but died there and according to Covenanting belief, would be whipped off straight to the nether regions. This history caught up with Cunninghame-Graham when he was addressing a political meeting.

'Whit aboot Bliddy Clavers?' shouted a heckler.

'Why don't you go to Hell and ask him?' retorted 'Don Roberto'.

When I was reporting the 'Cooncil', there was as much enmity between the Independent Labour Party and the official Labour Party as between the Labourites and the Progressives, who were regarded as Tories under an 'alias' — or 'an alibi', as one Socialist used to put it.

So when I.L.P.-er Jimmy Carmichael asked in the Chamber: 'Is this school pond exclusive tae the pupils or free fur all?' he brought the reply from Labour man Bailie J. M. Biggar: 'Mr Carmichael can have a bath if he requires one.' The Lord Provost intervened: 'We must have order.'

Bailie Biggar eventually became Lord Provost. At the same time there was a Provost called Mann, a diminutive but outspoken fellow, in neighbouring Rutherglen, now, most reluctantly, part of the city.

In a speech in Rutherglen Town Hall, a local patriot declaimed: 'Glasgow's Proavist may be Biggar, but thank Goad we hiv goat a Mann.'

Politics seems to have been altogether more enjoyable in those days, when there were so many splinter groups, especially on the Left, accusing one another of 'leadin the workers up the gerrdin' and being 'oot fur tae split the Labour Movement'.

James Maxton, that great Clydesider and I.L.P. worthy, was saying: 'We all know the Labour Party is a Tory sham and the Communists are playing the Tory game.'

What fun Glasgow Green could be! Will Fyffe's stage patter as a 'common old working chap' was hardly an exaggeration.

'Murder, murder, polis, three sterrs up.'

Glasgow children have the usual skipping rhymes and rhymes for 'stoattie' (bouncing the ball), but they favour also some rhymes which are perhaps more expressive of the old rough-and-tumble, 'stramash' and 'stushie' of life in the tenements.

Once, talking to some secondary school ('coamprensive' is the word now) children, I asked them what were their favourite poems. A boy stood up and recited solemnly:

> 'As Ah wiz walkin doon the sterr,
> Ah met a man that wiznae there.
> He wiznae there again the-day—
> Ah wish tae hang he'd go away.'

I was discussing my daily newspaper poems and the problems of rhyming generally, and I told them that there were no rhymes for 'oranges' or 'month'. The boys, however, would not be 'bate'. One of them gave me:

> 'The twelfth of a year is a month
> And the half of a tooth is a wunth.'

Another produced something with a real Clydeside flavour which ought to be in all the anthologies:

> 'A boabby catched us stealin oranges:
> Sez he tae us, "Noo mind Ah've warned yiz!"'

Another of their favourite rhymes, so different from the atmosphere of Robert Louis Stevenson's *Child's Garden of Verses* or A. A. Milne's 'Christopher Robin is saying his prayers', was:

> 'Murder, murder, polis, three sterrs up:
> The wumman in the toap flet hut me wi a cup.'
> (The woman in the top flat hit me with a cup.)

In the middle of the last war the cheeky boys were teasing our harassed tramway and bus conductresses with:

> 'Grup rem sterrs,
> Cleck rem ferrs,
> An' dinnae come doon fur honey perrs.'
> (Get up those stairs,
> Collect those fares,
> And don't come down for honey pears!')

'Honey perrs', a street fruit-vendor's cry, was for some obscure reason the cat-call of the Forties.

In the year leading up to the war, when gas-masks were first being distributed to the city children, their 'skipping sang' was:

> 'Underneath the spreading chessnut tree,
> Mr Chamberlain said tae me:
> "If ye want tae get yer gas-mask free,
> Come an' jine the A.R.P."'

Brawling schoolboys crowding on to buses on their way to school often provoke lectures from the conductress:

'Noo then yous boays, show yer brochtupness (up-bringing)! Yer murras wid be black affrontit at yiz, so they wid. That's if oany o yiz ivver hud murras (That is, if any of you ever had mothers).'

'Come oan, get aff!' she will say to the boy who has been told the bus is full up. It always seems a contradiction in terms.

'Come oan, noo, yous in front, move up ra bus rerr! Tak yer time, yous, lit rurra passengers get aff (Let the other passengers get off)! Ye dinnae need tae keep dingin rat bell: ra driver's no coarn-beef (deaf)! An' dinnae you set up yer neb tae craw me doon, Baw-face! Ah'm no yin o yer murra's skivvies (one of your mother's servants). Sa help ma Goad, ra public's ma warst enemy, an' thur wanes are pains.'

It is hard work handling Glasgow children. 'Ay, an' Ah only get them gaun tae the skill (school) an' comin' hame. Peety ra perr teachers! (Pity the poor teachers!) An' nae wunner their murras are gled tae be oot at some joab. Even washin sterrs wid be better nor bringin up wanes.'

When they lived in the old tenements with their 'backs' or courtyards in which the children played, the wee ones would often call up to their windows: 'Maw, throw iz doon a piece!' or, more roughly: 'Chuck iz doon a chit, Maw!'

A 'piece' or a 'chit' was what Kenn Dodd from Knotty Ash calls a 'buttie' — a sandwich or slice of bread, usually a jam sandwich, known in Glasgow as a 'jeely piece'. A 'chittery piece' (or chit) is the sandwich taken to the city swimming baths to be eaten after leaving the pond, when the child is 'chitterin' (shivering).

In a popular Glasgow story, one mother, importuned to throw down a sandwich, shouted into the 'back' in reply:

'Awa ootae there! Ye ken fine ye cannae get a chit the noo: yer Paw's at ra fitbaw wirra breid-knife!' (Your father is at the football with the bread-knife.)

Glasgow likes to tell stories against itself, especially on the themes of drink and violence, including hooliganism at 'ra ghemm' (the match).

But, apropos of the tradition of the piece thrown down from the tenement window, a folksong genius of today has composed a song which laments: 'Ye cannae throw doon pieces fae a twenty-storey hoose'.

Many of our children now live in high-rise flats and in their infancy are pitied as 'match-boax wanes', as often they have to play on landings in very confined space when their mothers are terrified to let them out to the play-grounds provided by well-meaning but purblind local authorities.

To revert to the bairn's piece, it is often jocosely called, by older Glas-wegians, a 'serr haun' (a sore hand). 'At's a richt serr haun ye've goat rerr', the 'wane' will be told as he struggles to keep his grip on an outsize 'chit' from a hard-bitten 'murra' with a 'hert' of gold — or perhaps just a desire to have peace.

Rosslyn Mitchell, a Glasgow city councillor who had been an M.P. (he defeated Mr Asquith in a memorable Paisley by-election) was involved with Glasgow children evacuated to country districts at the time of the German air-raids, and he used to tell me of the revolution these early war-time moves created in the lives of these city 'wanes'.

One boy wrote to Glasgow from his rural retreat: 'It's lovely. What big stars they have here!'

One boy from Garnethill, who had had to labour up city braes in his home territory, commented sincerely to the councillor: 'It's great tae live whaur there's hills!' He meant green ones, not those covered with concrete.

Many a loving parent, however, must have been jealous of the way in which their new homes in the country had captured the hearts of these children from overcrowded conditions. Two of the evacuees, brothers who had been allowed home for Christmas and then taken back to the country, wrote to their parents with shocking candour: 'We are glad to get back to our beds again.'

Children are great customers of the wee sweetie-shops which, because they sell many different wares, from lemonade to fire-lighters, are called in Glasgow 'Jenny Awthings' or, if the proprietors are men, 'Joanny Awthings' ('awthing' means everything, a general description of their stock.)

Generations of Glasgow 'wanes' shopped for 'shugger bools' (sugar balls), 'chuch Jeans' (tough chewing toffee otherwise known as 'stickjaw'), and 'sugarally' (licorice). There is even a district in Glasgow known as the Sugarally Mountains. Now everything is packaged and the youngsters go in for things like 'tottie crisps', and as often as not the 'Joahnny Awthing' has a name like Mohammed or Abdul.

The children still use old Glasgow words for the parts of the street. They play 'bools' (marbles) sometimes along the 'syver' (the kerbside gutter) or sail paper boats along it till the water reaches the 'stank' (drain). A Glasgow schoolgirl writing that hardy annual, 'The Autobiography of a Penny', concluded:

'As luck would have it, I rolled along a syver and fell doon a stank.'

A schoolboy in another memorable essay wrote:

'The weasel is a cunning beast, and sleekit forbye.'

'Sleekit' (slicked and shinny) means the same as cunning or furtive. It occurs in Burns's 'To a Mouse': 'Wee, sleekit, cowrin', tim'rous beastie...'

One boy called in at a public library, looking for one of the volumes of Conan Doyle's immortal Sherlock Holmes series.

'I'm sorry,' said the librarian, 'all the Sherlock Holmes books seem to be out.'

'Jist gie me wan o Rob Roy's!' said the boy.

Another lad asked the same librarian: 'Hiv ye goat the *Book of Aquaria*?'

'Yes, my boy, what do you want it for?'

''Cause ma mither has bocht a goldfish an' waants tae ken hoo tae feed it.'

45

For generations Glasgow children have gone to 'swarees' or evening treats organised by religious and educational bodies, notably the Band of Hope, the Rechabites and other worthy institutions designed to keep the young on the strait and narrow.

Usually the youngster passed the doorman who checked his ticket, and farther along the passageway there was some lady or gentleman handing out paper bags (known in Glasgow as 'pokes') containing perhaps a pie and a bun or a piece of cake, to be eaten later with a cup of tea, in an interval between elevating films or lantern lectures.

In Glasgow newspaper lore is preserved the story of an editor who was sent two tickets for a soiree. As his staff were fully occupied that evening, he thought that, for a treat, he and his wife would go along.

A huge retired policeman was doing duty at the other door. The editor handed over his tickets in anticipation of a V.I.P. welcome. The doorman scanned the tickets and shouted along the corridor to the man at the inner door, who was handing out the pies and cookies: 'Press! Nae poke!' No food for the V.I.P's!

Often, on leaving, the children were given an orange at the door.

Another childhood memory of Glaswegians is fishing for 'baggy mennens' (sticklebacks) and 'berdies' (beardies or loach). Sometimes with luck they even caught a 'trootie' (small trout) or a 'braize' (bream). They also collected tadpoles and hoped they would become 'puddocks' (frogs).

'Onybody here fae Paisley? We need a corkscrew.'

'We've come tae Edinburgh fae wur city in the West,
We've walked the length o Princes Street and wurnae much
        impressed:
We visitit ra Castle and we done ra Royal Mile,
But give iz ra Gorbals ivvery time an' Merryhill
        fur style!

'We're ra boays, ra boanny wee boays fae Glasgow,
We huv saw yer city an' we hink it's a fiasco:
Aw ra famous places at ra Yankee tourists ask o
Couldnae haud a caunle tirra Jamaica Brig in Glasgow.

'We went intae a restyoorant tae hae a spoat o nosh:
We didnae unnerstaun thum whun they stertit talkin
        posh:
A waitress cam and assed us: "Will ye huv it *à la carte?*"
We answered, "Naw, we'll think we'll hae a barra-load
        tae start."

'We're ra boays, ra boanny wee boays fae Glasgow,
We huv saw yer city an' we hink it's a fiasco:
Aw ra famous places at ra Yankee tourists ask o
Couldnae haud a caunle tirra Jamaica Brig in Glasgow.

Glasgow cherishes its image as the friendliest city in the world. It reads
with pleasure the Press which perpetuates that legend and it hears with
approval the many comments to this effect on radio and television.

Just as fixed are its citizens' stereotypes about other towns, and especially
about Edinburgh. 'Edinburgh's the capital,' they say, 'but Glasgow *has* the
capital.' And they are especially critical about two things in Edinburgh —
its 'werra' (weather) and its allegedly toffee-nosed inhabitants, the 'Geichs':

'See Embruh? Thoan's an awfae caul place, intit? Noo Glesca is shumid,
but Embruh's no fit fur shuman beans, no unless Eskimoes. Bress puggies
(monkeys) is no in it.'

'See Poartabella? It wid be rerr furra Ferr if it wiznae fur thoan eass win
(east wind). Ye cannae get sittin oana sauns (on the sands) furra win blawn
in yer face. Cannae even get eatin yer pokey hat (ice-cream cone).'

Portobello, Edinburgh's seaside resort, was so popular with Glaswegians
before they discovered they could get fish and chips on the Costa Brava, that
at one time during Glasgow Fair Fortnight ('ra Ferr') families were sleeping
on the sands, a real test of 'rawerra' (the weather) or of the Glasgow folk's
adaptability.

'See thae Embruh folk? They're as caul as their toon, so they are. Goad's
Frozen People, sure'n they are. Jivver hear about ra Glesca man at shook
hauns wirra Embruh man? He loass fowrae iz fing-urs wi froassbite.' (Lost
four of his fingers with frostbite).

'Ye kin haurly get speakin tae them oan a bus even, they're that toffee-
nosed. See we Glesca folk?'

(It is always '*wee* Glesca folk', never '*us* Glesca folk'. Alasdair Dunnett,
ex-Editor of *The Scotsman*, a Glasgow man, used to crack: 'What about *big*
Glasgow folk?')

'See we Glesca folk? Noo we're different awragirra (altogether). We meet a flah, we speak tae um, whirra he's black, white or yella. We're no stuck-up, like.

'But see thae Embruh folk? Ye'd need a innerduction, so ye wid. They nivver open their mooths till they've kent ye aboot a week. No that ye could unnerstaun them if they ivver dae speak, wi their Panloaf Moarnside paa'er.

'Ass thum the road tirra Waverley an they'll luck at ye as if ye wiz a Dalek or sumpn. They hink y're sayin: "Tak me tae yer leader!" so they div.'

'Moarnside' (Morningside) is the district in Edinburgh which corresponds in legend to Kelvinside in Glasgow. Its inhabitants are popularly supposed to speak an even more intensive Panloaf than the rest of the Edinburgh citizens.

In fact there is a lot of broad Scots spoken in Morningside, and in Edinburgh generally, but the inhabitants of the capital always put on their best English when talking to strangers, including 'gents' from Glasgow.

'Noo we Glesca folk are different awragirra. Come intae Glesca an' we spoat right away ye're a stranger an' right away we're oot tae gie ye a helpin haun. We'll say "Tak wan o thae green an yella wans" — ra busses, ken? — an' "Murrawell — at's a rid wan doon at ra Croass. Embruh's a green wan. Mulguy's a blue wan fae Buchanan Street. Try ra Subway, but: ra Unnerground, like! It's ra bess urra loat (the best of the lot), so it is. Yiz kin get jissaboot onywhaur on them Blue Trains, but." At's *us* — information while yiz wait.'

This is a boast one must acknowledge to be justified. Glaswegians *are* very friendly to strangers, and very willing to tell you about their city, of which they are extremely proud.

'Thur owre much talk aboot Embruh being sae boanny an' aw rat. It's nae boannier nor Glesca. An' Ah'll tell ye sumpn fur nuh-hin (something for nothing): Embruh's goat worse slums nor Glesca. The only difference is — through there, they hide them doon ra back streets.

'Histoaric? Glesca's jiss as histoaric as Embruh. But it's no sae herrymowlit (hairy-mouldy). Ken whit Embruh is, wi its "histoaric"? It's foosty, so it is.'

'Foosty' means so mouldy you can smell the 'foost', the indescribable smell of mouldiness.

'D'ye ken whit Ah hink? That's hoo Embruh folk aye lucks as if they're feelin a smell.'

When people are stand-offish in Glasgow and have a supercilious expression, they are said to 'aye luck as if they're feeling a smell' (always look as if they are smelling someting unpleasant). In Scotland we do not smell a smell — we 'feel' it or 'fin' (find) it.

There are stereotypes about other towns and their aboriginals, but none so

'Princes Street's only hauf built: it's only goat wan side.'

strong as the ideas about Edinburgh. Rutherglen (called 'Ruglen'), which managed to resist absorption in the city of Glasgow and preserve its separate burgh status until the recent municipal reorganisation, is regarded affectionately as 'aul-farran' (old-fashioned) and a close community.

'Ah ken folk in Ruglen at's been there fur twa-three generations an' they're still cawed ''in-comers''. At's a fact, as fack's daith (as true as death). Yer folk hiz tae uv been livin in Ruglen fae the Middle Ages afore ye're acceppit as a Ruglonian. Ay, unless they cam there wi Wallace the Bruce, ye've hud it, china. Ye're nuhhin but an ''In-comer'', an' in Ruglen that's you hud yer chips, so it is.'

Despite this, Glaswegians are disposed to be benevolent to Ruglonians, and if they meet them in Edinburgh they are prepared to claim them as their own.

'Efter aw, we're aw Joack Tamson's berrns.'

'Ruglen's wee roon rid lums reek briskly' is a tongue-twister, like 'The Leith Police dismisseth us', and it became a song much sung in Glasgow pantomimes and expressing the citizens' affectionate regard for this country-looking town on its outskirts.

'Sno a bad wee toon. Ken something? Ah'd rether hae Ruglen's Main Street nor thoan Princes Street in Embruh. Oh, Sauchiehall Street ivvery time! At's like the Stran in London, ken? Or the Champs Leezie in Paris — Ah've been there, ye ken — ay, an' the Coo Dam in Berlin whun Ah wiz in the Army. But if Ah didnae huv Sauchiehall Street Ah'd shinner hae Main Street, Ruglen, nor oany o yer Princes Streets. Fur a stert, Princes Street's only hauf built: it's only goat wan side, ye could say. But Main Street's like Sauchie — it's goat shoaps baith sides.'

Sauchiehall Street's name originally meant a willow-strewn marshland, Sauchie Haugh. But now there is no water there except what falls from the sky on those who take advantage of the pedestrian precinct, or what gets into 'ra bevvy' (the drink), and the only thing willowy about the place is 'ra wee smashers swankin their tottie alang' the street of streets.

At the other side of the city from Rutherglen lies the substantial town of Paisley, almost a city on its own, and about Paisley folk also there are legends. Unlike Rutherglen, it still resists engulfment in Glasgow, though it is tied to it like a 'Symees' twin.

Paisley has an abbey and other beautiful buildings, and has always been praised for its diversification in industry and commerce. Now it has a College of Technology which rivals Glasgow's two universities. But older Glaswegians still remember the Paisley folk as 'corks'.

'Oanybody here fae Paisley? We need a coarkscrew!' used to be the call on the trains and the Clyde pleasure-steamers, as in Glasgow legend Paisley men always carried cork-screws in the hope, it was alleged, that this would win them a share in the bottle they so kindly opened.

There is another legend about Paisley which I have heard discussed humorously among literary Glaswegians. This is to the effect that every Paisley native is a poet.

At a dinner in the town, so it is said, when someone proposed the toast of 'The Poets of Paisley', no one stood up. They all thought they were included in the toast.

Paisley folk are affectionately called 'buddies' by Glaswegians — and by themselves.

The name originated when an indignant minister in the town rebuked some girls for coming in late to the service: 'Ay, ye come wauchlin in here hauf-an-oor late, hopin awbody will pey attention tae ye, an' you aw dressed up an' poothert an' pentit tae gie the impression ye're Edinburgh leddies, whun awbody here kens fine ye're jist Paisley buddies (persons).'

Now, with the American language brought in by the media infecting our local dialects, 'buddies' may be understood as meaning 'chums'. That suits the Paisley people all right. So long as they are given a special place in the affection of the Glaswegians.

To be liked by people who 'think theirsels nae sheepshank banes' (consider themselves no leg-of-mutton bones, or in other words, 'fancy theirsels nae en') is always gratifying.

Of Aberdonians, Glaswegians believe 'they're no sae gruppy (mean) as they mak theirsels oot tae be — at's aw a tale, ken?' Dundonians they hardly know, but are prepared to consider 'gey like wursels'. People from the Port of Leith are warmly regarded, perhaps because Leith dislikes being part of Edinburgh.

'Here a darky gonny dae tricks.'

A private of the Highland Light Infantry approaching his camp after dark heard the challenge: 'Halt! Who goes there?'

'A Scoatch soadger,' he shouted in reply.

'Sing "Scoats Wha Hae"!' ordered the sentry.

'Ach! Ah dinnae ken ra words.'

'Advance, Joack, an' be recognised!'

The H.L.I. (nicknamed 'ra Herry-Leggit Irishmen') are now amalgamated with the Ayrshire regiment, the Royal Scots Fusiliers, in the Royal Highland Fusiliers, but most of the soldier stories in Glasgow are about the H.L.I. and

51

their kilted battalion, the Glasgow Highlanders.

A contingent of H.L.I. travelled for many miles in railway horse-boxes without any hint, among the rank and file, of their destination. They made it after dark, pitched their tents and lay down to sleep.

In the morning the 'wee nyaff', who always gets up before his 'chinas' and has to go round exploring, wandered around until he came upon a Moslem laying out a prayer-mat, as it happened to be a predominantly Mohammedan country into which their troop train had conveyed them.

Excitedly, the 'wee nyaff' rushed back to his tent, and woke his comrades with the cry: 'Heh, yous, come oot here quick or ye'll miss yersels! Here a darky gonny dae tricks.' (Here is a coloured gentleman about to perform acrobatics.)

It was an H.L.I. man in France in the Great War of 1914-18 who discovered how easy it was for a Scotsman to speak French. 'Ah went up tae the ferm, like, an' thur this madatmasel comes oot an' Ah jist says tae her ''Twa oofs''. The silly bizzim gies me three eggs, an' Ah gies her wan back. As easy as fawin aff a dyke.'

Another H.L.I. man in the same war was chatting up a mademoiselle, who had learned to speak, not Franglais, but Frécossais, and who repulsed his advances with 'Scotch sodger, no bon'.

'Whit a bloomin cheek!' he exposulated. 'Oors is the best bawn (band) in the British Army.'

Not all wearers of the tartan, in the kilt or in the trews, appreciate the finer music of the pipes. Marches, reels and strathspeys are all right, but the pibroch, or *piobaireachd*, as they spell it in Gaelic, is to these as Beethoven to the Beatles, and it is only the Highland *aficionados* who know what it is all about.

A first-class piper in the Royal Highland Fusiliers was walking slowly up and down the barrack square practising a slow pibroch for a piping competition. Two of his regimental comrades, young 'fluhs', were standing by.

One asked the other: 'Whissie daein?' (What is he doing?)

'Ach!' replied the second private: 'He's jist tunin' his pipes.'

To confuse the stranger, the Royal 'Highland' Fusiliers, like the H.L.I. before them, are classed as a 'Lowland' Regiment.

At manoeuvres in the Southern Uplands near Glasgow, an officer told a private of the Fusiliers, who had taken cover in a slit trench: 'Tell that man up there to get off the skyline!'

The private replied: 'Oh, at's no a man, sir: at's oor serjint.' (That's not a man: that's our sergeant.)

Another regiment with a strong Glasgow connection is the Argyll and Sutherland Highlanders. The Argylls were stationed in Jamaica when I was out there in the late Twenties.

I was in the lounge of a pub at Half-Way Tree, near Kingston, Jamaica, when I heard a loud male duet from the adjoining saloon: 'Ra Boannie Wells o Wearie.'

I walked through and there were two kilted Glaswegians 'giving it laldy' singing an Edinburgh song which they fondly believed to be a Glasgow one: otherwise, I am sure they would never have sung it.

When I greeted them at the end of their chorus, one turned to the other and told him, as if he were Sherlock Holmes demonstrating his powers of deduction to Dr Watson: 'Scoatch!'

Although for generations we littérateurs have been trying to establish 'Scots' and 'Scottish' in place of the word 'Scotch' (which, incidentally, was used by Burns, Scott and Robert Louis Stevenson, all good Scots writers), the populace — and not only in Glasgow — sticks resolutely to 'Scoatch' and 'Scoa'ish'.

If you called a Scot a 'Scotchman' he would not be offended, unless he happened to be a 'skillteacher', terribly educated or 'weel pitten-oan'.

A private of the Argylls in Jamaica, a typical young Glaswegian, was standing on 'sentry-go' when his commanding officer passed. He sprang to attention and gave the orthodox salute but added the friendly Glasgow touch: 'Anither het day, Curnel!'

Two Glasgow members of the Home Guard sitting in a slit trench on the city's outskirts in the last war were discussing the shattering news that the Low Countries had been invaded by the Germans and the French had capitulated. One veteran said to the other with a profound nod: 'Ay, Wullie, it's gonny be a lang war if thae English gie in.'

When Anthony Eden proclaimed the formation of the L.D.V. (Local Defence Volunteers, though we interpreted it as 'Likely tae Develop Varicose'), I put my name down, as instructed, with my local police. I was resident in 'Free Rutherglen', which ran its own affairs, and was policed by the Lanarkshire Constabulary.

I waited for what I considered rather a long time without hearing any more about the L.D.V., and I published a paragraph to this effect in my Glasgow paper.

The result was a phone-call from a carpet merchant off George Square, Glasgow, who said: 'I can't understand your story. My company of Local Defence Volunteers are already drilling in Maryhill Barracks, and you are welcome to join us.'

So I began my heroic Home Guard career in a Glasgow squad, square-bashing in the H.L.I.'s barracks and with a rifle drawn from the H.L.I. armoury.

We were not a very inspiring bunch — a kind of 'Chanty-wrasslers' Rifles'. We had at least one man who did not know his right foot from his left, and we had another who had an artificial leg.

One wee Glasgow man summed it up. It happened that there were a few Luftwaffe prisoners in the barracks, in transit to their prison camp, and they passed us, under escort, carrying loaves of bread to their quarters. They were the tallest, heftiest and handsomest of Germans, and they studied us with amusement as they were marched past. My wee neighbour remarked to me:

'Ah hope tae Goad thae blighters dinnae think we're in the Army! If they see *shachly wee bachles* like *us* drillin here, they'll imagine Britain's ready tae chuck it in.'

At that stage we still had no uniforms — nothing but 'L.D.V.' brassards — but at least we were not drilling with walking sticks, brooms or pikes. Luckily, prisoners' mail would be censored.

Shortly afterwards I received my instructions to report for duty to the Rutherglen battalion and my drilling at Maryhill ceased.

One of my young Lanarkshire comrades — an apprentice 'brickie' (bricklayer) — was out on patrol one night in a barren field near Glasgow called the 'Sodey (Soda) Waste', and he came back with the exciting tale: 'Ah thocht Ah fan (thought I found) a land-mine stickin oot the grun. It turnt oot tae be a three-leggit poat, but Ah kicked it tae mak sherr (to make sure).'

On the famous morning when all the Defence Forces of Britain were stood to, in September 1940, we found ourselves manning road blocks on the western approach to Glasgow just on the Rutherglen side of Shawfield Park, the greyhound racing stadium and football ground belonging to Clyde Football Club (known in Glasgow as 'ra Bully Wee').

Towards dawn some of my comrades on patrol discovered that a Glasgow Home Guard company were sitting pretty inside Clyde's headquarters, with all the kitchen facilities, more than necessary for the universal war-time practice of 'brewin-up' (making cups of tea).

We had no idea what was happening in the country at large. We stopped men at the road blocks as they walked or cycled to work and each man we challenged brought us a new rumour of Germans landing by parachute, some with rubber dinghies for our inland waterways!

We were hourly expecting to have to tackle Max Schmeling or some other hefty German paratrooper. We 'shachly wee bachles'!

One of our platoon was a young Glasgow business man who resided in our suburb of Burnside, and who had recently married. His wife was always anxious about him, so he made a point of wangling the patrol which would take him near his home, where he could slip in for a cup of tea and be able to comfort his new bride.

On the morning of the 'invasion' he was one of those who had penetrated to the Glasgow mob's 'cushy' quarters. As well as being able to enjoy a cup of tea he discovered there was a phone handy, so he proceeded to phone up his ever-loving wife. One of his comrades overheard the phone-call and repeated it with relish to the rest of us:

'He tellt his wife no tae worry but there wiz Germans floating aboot in rubber dinghies on Loch Lomond, but he thocht he'd be hame for his brekfist.'

The Royal Scots Fusiliers were known as the 'Fusilier Joacks'. Although an 'Errshire' (Ayrshire) regiment, they attracted young Glaswegians. George II, the last British monarch to command an army in battle, saw the Fusiliers in action at Dettingen. He told their C.O., Sir Andrew Askew of Lochnaw: 'I was sorry to see the French cavalry get in among your men today, Colonel.' Sir Andrew gave a typically Scottish reply: 'Oh ay, your Majesty, but they didnae get oot again.'

As they were originally raised by the Earl of Mar and wore grey trousers, they were known also as 'Mar's Greybreeks.'

Piper John McLaughlin of the H.L.I., at the Battle of Badajoz, got a bullet through the bag of his pipes and sat on a gun carriage to repair them, rightly regarding them to be a weapon of war.

You will find Glaswegians in almost every Scottish regiment. And many who have fought alongside them will tell you: 'Thae wee nyaffs are the best o the lot. They dinnae ken when they're bate.'

In Lanarkshire we proudly wore, on our forage caps, and later on our Kilmarnock bonnets, the mullet and bugle badge of the Cameronians (Scottish Rifles).

The Lanarkshire regiment also has its quota of Glaswegians. A German restaurateur found an equivalent for 'wee nyaffs' when his bar was wrecked by some Cameronians. He called them 'poison dwarfs', and the phrase was enthusiastically picked up by the Glasgow Press.

'Ay, Ah ken you: ye gie me aw the bamsticks.'

Sport in Glasgow as elsewhere has developed its own technical jargon. Go to 'ra fitbaw', 'ra dugs' (greyhound racing), or 'ra bookie', and you have to learn the lingo. The same applies on higher levels to 'bools' (bowling) and 'gowff, goff or golf'.

In the first three of these sports, and probably in the fourth, however, you will find similar references to 'bamsticks'. This is a definitely working-class word which applies with equal severity to 'chinas', shop stewards, branch secretaries of unions, politicians, 'ra plerrs' (the players) at 'fitbaw' — naturally along with the linesmen and the referee — the 'dugs' which one backs, and which fall behind in the race for various real and suspected reasons, and 'ra cuddies'.

Horses are properly called 'hoarses'. The word 'cuddy' means a donkey, but as many of the noble steeds turn out to be 'bamsticks' one is being almost polite to call them 'cuddies'. Some of them plainly — or their jockeys — would have a better chance in a 'dunkie race' on the 'sauns'.

'Ay, Ah ken you: ye gie me aw the bamsticks.' I heard an aul wife tell a man in Argyle Street. I never found out whether it was horses or dogs he dealt in, but obviously he was that arch-bamstick, the duff tipster. The horses and dogs such unreliable prophets handed out to their associates used to be called simply 'stumers', but 'bamstick' is an umbrella term for everything and everyone that lets you down.

The horses run far away at 'Err', Musselburgh, Market Rasen, Newmarket, and so the punter (who is sometimes, though we never dare mention this, a bit of a 'bamstick' in his own right — or wrong) has not the same opportunity of working out what happened to his bet on the course.

TV helps a bit, perhaps, but there are more opportunities to go bonkers at the sight of one's bet going down the 'syver' and the 'stank' at the greyhound stadium, and there a lot of punters advance theories about the cause of the disaster.

'Somebody musta gien that dug a pie!'

'Naw, it jiss wiznae a greyhound. It hiz legs like a dashhound.'

'It diznae ken a herr whun it sees yin.'

'It wiz yersel at picked it, but.'

'No really. Ah goat thoan Ken Awthing tae mark ma kerd. He kens Sweet Fanny. He kens as much aboot dugs as ma hin-en kens aboot astroanomy.'

You come away wondering who Ken Awthing and Sweet Fanny can be.

But it is at the 'ghemm' — the football match — that you really hear the aficionados at their best. They know so much about the intricacies of the sport that it is a wonder more of them do not land high-salaried jobs as managers or trainers.

In Glasgow they are mostly concerned about the respective merits of 'ra Aul Firm' — 'ra Boays in Blue' and 'ra Cel'ic'. Some may give their support to Queen's Park, 'ra Bully Wee' (Clyde), Partick Thistle or even Rutherglen Glencairn, but most of the city's sporting life revolves around Celtic and Rangers ('the Gers'). If you are a man at all, you are either a Rangers or a Celtic supporter: to support neither team is tantamount to confessing to agnosticism.

Among the true partisans, enthusiasm is expressed in strong terms. 'Follow, follow, we will follow Rangers!' and, on the other side, in calling Celtic Park 'Paradise'. For most of the season, of course, for a Celtic supporter it *is* Paradise, but for Rangers fans it is more like what Glasgow children call 'ra Burnin Fire'.

Whatever their persuasion, the fans are all experts:

'Did ye see that? The big mug! Lit a third-rate plerr tak it aff him, like takkin sugarally aff a wane!'

'Oaffside, ref! Whit the blazes are ye playin at? Ye're bookin ra wrang man.'

'Awaw ya daftie! Gie ra baw tae somebody at kin kick it! Cut oot ra fancy stuff an' gie'z a goal, ya clown!'

'They wid drive ye oot yer mine, so they wid.'

'See at leff hauf! He's jiss gettin in ra bloomin road.'

'Sell um tae America!'

'Play ra ghemm, ref!'

'See at stricken linesman! It's no a flag he should be kerryin, it's a white stick.'

'Ay, it's a guide-dug he's needin.'

'Owre ra line an' back in play an' he nivver seen it! Ay, Ah should think sae! Could ye no huv saw it fur yersel, insteed o huvvin tae hae it pyntit oot, but?'

'Ra plerrs is as blin as ra linesmen.'

'Ra baw went clean through his bowlie legs!'

'At's a boay! Pass it tae Joansin! *He* kin use it. Ay, boanny, Joansin, boanny! At's a beaut! Aw, crivvens, he's hut ra bliddy croassbaur!'

'Blooter thum, boays! At's a ticket fur peas-brose!'

'Pelt it in ra poke!'

No wonder the ebullient 'fitbaw wri'ers' for the Glasgow Sunday Press write so picturesquely. They are trying to match the constant witticisms of the 'terrace Tams' and 'Se'urday Sawnies'.

'Wan thing aboot you, Wullie: naebody wid say ye wiz bigotit.'

'Naw — I dinnae kerr wha wins. Ah dinnae gie a doaken, like, sae lang as they're aw in blue jerseys.'

Someone must have originated that phrase, but it must have been a long time ago.

'At's a ticket at last, ref. Oot wi ra ruddy crime-sheet!'

'Ach, ye've went an' booked ra wrang man, but!'

'Err at bamstick again — huddin oan tae ra baw as if he wiz ra only plerr in ra team.'

'Hinks he kin steal ra show, like ra wee dug at ra flea-circus (like the little dog at the flea-circus).'

'Selpmaboab! He coulda pitten it in ra poke his-sel an' he passes it back tae a man at wiznae there! Ay, hing yer heid in shame! Ah should think sae! Ye'll nivver get a chance like that again.'

'Dig a hole, ref!'

'Gie it tae Jardine... Aw, fur oany favour!'

'Come oan noo, Paurlane, it's aw yours. Shoot! In ra bag! Goavy-dick, it's awa fur ile (away for oil, wide of the mark).'

Rangers and Celtic supporters are born, not made. As one blue-sashed young man put it:

'Ma farra taught me tae sing whun Ah wiz at ma murra's knee:

> 'Oh Cherlie Shaw
> He nivver saw
> Whaur Alan Morton
> Pit ra baw.'

It is many years since Charlie Shaw failed to see where Alan Morton put the ball, but the record is almost Biblical.

Another Rangers supporter expostulated:

'Dinnae you be thinkin' it's jist the scruff at follas thur twa teams! Some o us is even toffs.' He added with a bashful laugh: 'No *me*, but.'

'Fitbaw poalitics' are discussed away from the field, and form the stock-in-trade also of the Sunday Press writers. In this sphere, again, the Old Firm takes up most of the space.

In the pubs they solemnly discuss these affairs of state:

'They should nivveruv lit Joack Steen go sooth.'

'Naw, it's like floggin the National Moanyament tae ra English.'

(Jock Stein - who joins everyone else in pronouncing his name 'Steen' — did in fact become the manager of the Scottish national team, so all ended well.)

'Awrasame, Ah hink Billy McNeill'll prove his-sel jiss as big a maun as Joack Steen.'

'At remains tae be Steen,' cracks the supporters' club comic, but the joke is considered in bad taste and does not get a laugh in this serious-minded circle. These Celtic supporters can be very solemn, even when they are on a winning streak:

'Look at Fir Park err! We blootert Murrawell, sure'n we did. Five-wan's no tae be sneezed at.'

'Ay, but thoan wiz nae walk-owre, wiz it noo? Ah didnae like ra wey ra Murrawell plerrs wiz gettin through.'

'Right enough! Ah wiznae awfae happy masel, that first hauf. Ah felt like gaun hame at hauf-time whun Edvaldsson hung wan oan his ain goalie, an' gien Murrawell ra equalizer. It ferr pit ma watter aff ra bile, so it did.'

'Ah, but wizn' thoan a boaby-dazzler fae Glavin, right intae Alfie Conn's barra? An' ra wan he passed tae Aitken fur anurra wan, as shin as they goat stertit again?'

Concern about the eyesight of officials and participants is not confined to soccer fans. Fight aficionados also are frequently exasperated by optical deficiency.

I was in the Caledonian Market one night watching a fight between Jim Campbell and a little Japanese. This was long before Pearl Harbour.

Jim Campbell was a capable Glasgow flyweight, who used to go round in those days offering to back himself against his world champion townsman, Benny Lynch. Benny did not take up the challenge.

Against the Jap, Jim lost the decision on points. The referee, an old chap called Bill Strelly, was hooted out of the ring.

He sat down beside me, highly indignant at the crowd's reaction, and he said to me out of the side of his mouth: 'Ah dinnae gie a doaken if they're black, white, yella or green, the best man wins, sae faur as Ah'm coancerned.'

The spectators were not being racial, only locally patriotic. Also they were convinced that Bill had given a 'rank bad' decision.

Hardly had the two fighters reached their dressing-rooms when the Master of Ceremonies was in the ring announcing the next match. When he added: 'And your referee, ladies and gentlemen, is that popular Glasgow sportsman, Mr William Strelly,' you could hear a brick drop! Mr Strelly's fellow citizens booed and hissed until the next bout got started.

It was scarcely under way before one of the boxers stepped back suddenly, and Strelly, who was immediately behind him, had to sidestep rapidly. Loud rang that voice from the back of the hall:

'Watch the blin man!'

There is not so much use of the vernacular in golfing circles, although some of the old worthies, such as James Braid, were famous for their broad Scots sayings.

It is usually the free-lance caddie, who may be a city youth, who is credited with phrases in the language of the people, such as the lad who was accused by his hirer of being too slow in handing over the proper clubs. He argued: 'Whidgie expeck fur whit you're peyin me? A flash o lightnin?'

And there was the youth who had failed to keep up a tyro's score but defended himself with 'It's no a caddie you waant — it's a chattert accoontant.'

Another was asked by a lady golfer: 'Do you think I could get home in seventy?' and replied: 'Ah dinnae ken whaur ye stey (I don't know where you reside).'

As for the popular sport of bowling ('bools'), it is one in which miming plays a greater part than speech. Especially picturesque are the dances of players trying to influence the bowl after it has left the hand.

'See at perr!' a spectator commented as he watched mixed doubles: 'Talk aboot Margot Fonteyn and Rudolf Nureyev!'

'Less face it, Mac, ye cannae win.'

Inevitably, since Glasgow is a city of the world, the purity of its speech is constantly threatened with infection from other world languages, including English.

Especially the American version. There is very little between Glasgow, on its west side, and the United States. As the commentator in the film, *Whisky Galore*, said of the Hebrides and the broad Atlantic: 'Nothing beyond that — only America!'

Glaswegians have been bombarded with American expressions for many generations. Over fifty years ago we were learning to say 'It gifs' from the comic papers featuring 'The Katzenjammer Kids', 'Dinty Moore's' and 'corned beef and cabbage' from 'Bringing Up Father' and 'I pay out a flock of dough to a bunch of bums' from 'Tillie the Toiler'.

Just before the talkies hit us with the full force of New York, Brooklynese and Californian (with East European adhesions), we had Jimmy Gleason's *Is Zat So?* On the stage, with the programme explaining what 'sock-peddler's pilot', 'I'll clean dat tramp like soap never did' and 'Did ya finally back

'See at perr! Talk about Margot Fonteyn and Rudolf Nureyev!'

away from da troff?' meant.

Before that, some of the sub-titles on the silent movies, or, as we called them, the 'picturs' or the 'fillums', educated us with such expressions as 'Cheese it, de cops!' and 'Ain't she the cat's pyjamas?'

American song-writers, enthusiastically plugged in sheet music at our seaside resorts, taught us a lot of American as well, before the talkies came with Al Jolson saying: 'Well, anyway, my mother likes me.'

Now Glasgow has two international airports, including the lifeline to America through Prestwick, and so it is a jet city. Also don't forget it was largely built up on the American trade in the days of the tobacco lords, and its port has always laid it open to American influence, as much as to those of Ireland and England.

So whatever the current phrase — the in-phrase — is, in the English-speaking world at large, you will hear its echoes around Goosedubs, Trongate, Townhead, Argyle and Sauchiehall, but usually in a Glasgow accent:

'Less face it, Mac, ye cannae win.'

'Ah couldnae kerr less.'

'Ah couldnae agree merr.'

The city also has in-phrases of its own. A Glasgow agent for a cold-type process told me: 'It's the greatest invention since sliced breid', and I have heard this wisecrack hundreds of times since.

A prevalent phrase these days, much used by shop stewards and branch secretaries in radio and TV interviews, is 'No way'. It has the force of 'We shall not be moved' and 'No passeran', and is indispensable now for the expression of the stiff-necked attitude considered necessary in industrial disputes.

'So does that mean that the strike will be called off?' asks the BBC or Scottish Television interviewer.

'No way,' replies the official.

'Is that not rather an obstructive attitude?'

'No coamment.'

It is refreshing to get away from these current clichés to some robust old Scottish saying, fortunately still preserved:

'There owre mony young unemployed waitin on deid men's shin.'

(Waiting on dead men's shoes.)

'Some o thae pundits, as they think theirsels, are aye wyce ahin-haun.'

(Always wise behind-hand.)

'This wife-swappin lark they keep speakin aboot — whaw wid niffer fur an aul yin?'

(Who would do a swap for an old one?)

62

'Caw cannie wi the butter!'

(Go easy with the butter: this was a popular phrase with our grand-parents, and was even printed on butter dishes. But most of us have forgotten that, as well as being an injunction to be economical with a scarce commodity, it meant: 'Cut out the flattery!' or as the current phrase has it: 'Flattery will get you nowhere.')

The invasion of in-words and phrases affects modes of address in the city.

Ladies strange to the Scottish tongue are sometimes perplexed if not offended to be addressed, by bus drivers and conductors, taxi-drivers, waitresses and shop assistants, as 'Dear!' or, most perplexing to non-Scots, 'Hen!'

But there seems to be even more undue familiarity in the latest form of address to ladies of all ages: 'Doll!' This is an obvious invader, but it has quickly taken root in the vocabulary of persons 'serving the public'.

Small boys in Glasgow at one time addressed strange elderly gentlemen as 'Maister!' but long ago this developed into 'Mister!' It is meant to be a polite term, equivalent to 'Sir!'

We were taught to address 'wumman skillteachers' as 'Miss' if they looked young enough and 'Ma'am' if they were rather mature.

Now, tolerant as I am of folk-ways, I find it disconcerting, if not down-right insulting, to be addressed as 'Jimmy!'

This shares the honours with 'Mac!' as the common way of addressing male strangers.

'Whit are ye luckin at, Jimmy?'

'Yer ferr's up, Jimmy.'

'Whissa time, Jimmy?'

Although most Glasgow working-men are soft-voiced and studiously polite in their approach, there is the aggressive type who uses 'Jimmy' in a hectoring tone, and with obvious intention to down-grade, to men who look like 'toffs' — collar-and-tie rather than blue-collar.

It may stem from the sailors' expression for the mate or some other senior officer — 'Jimmy the Wan' — which may originally have come from King James I, the jumped-up King James VI of Scotland.

Whatever its origin, I interpret 'Jimmy' as conveying: 'Dinnae you be thinkin ye're awbody, fur *Ah*'m some o thum!'

'Mac', in contrast, may even be complimentary in intent, suggesting that one is a member of a clan — Scots or Irish — and established in the community, a brother-Glaswegian perhaps, one of 'Joan Tamson's (or Jock Tamson's) bairns'.

'Whissa time, Mac?'

'Huv ye sich'n a hing as a light, Mac?'

'Kin Ah hae a dekko at yer paper, Mac? Jiss the racin section!'

While 'Jimmy' usually to me suggests a chip on the user's shoulder, 'Mac', though perhaps lacking in respect, is usually friendly, and is best taken in that spirit. As a wise Gaelic scholar has said: 'Blessed are the meek, for they shall inherit the earth, and anyone who has studied Irish or Scottish Gaelic will tell you that "Meek" (*Mic*) is the plural of *Mac*.'

The handling of Christian name or surname usually indicates the degree of familiarity. 'Shooy' is the usual form for Hugh, but you may call him 'Shug' if you are a close 'china'.

Glaswegians in their 'hooker-doon bunnets' and tartan 'grauvits' used to be typified as 'Haw Wull!' A visiting London journalist once told me: 'Everybody in Glasgow seems to be called "Wullie".' It is very nearly true.

The Rt. Hon. William Ross, during his reign as Secretary of State for Scotland, was universally known, both in derision and in respect, as 'Wullie Roass', and a popular cartoon figure in the *Sunday Post* is the wee boy called 'Oor Wullie', featured next door to 'The Broons' (our way of saying the Browns).

Alexander in Glasgow is usually shortened to 'Alex' — not 'Alec' as is the Edinburgh style — but you sometimes get 'Ellick', 'Eck', 'Sandy' or 'Sawny'. Another popular cartoon figure is 'Se'urday Sawny' (Saturday Sandy), the archetypal Glasgow football fan. The Gaelic form, Alasdair, is usually shortened to 'Ally'.

Peter (pronounced at best 'Pee'er' with that elusive Scots *t*) is often reduced to 'Pate'.

Many a Glasgow James is familiarly addressed as 'Hamish' — the pronunciation of the Gaelic equivalent, *Seumas*, when used as a form of address.

'David' is usually 'Dave' or 'Davie', but sometimes it gets its old Scottish 'Sunday' form, 'Dauvit'. This marks the user as distinctly 'aul-farran'.

The most numerous, the Johns, get 'Jeck' and 'Jack' as often as 'Joack'. Kenneths are 'Ken' or 'Kenny', Rodericks 'Roddie' or 'Rory' (from the Gaelic form, *Ruaraidh*), Roberts are 'Rab', 'Rob' or 'Boab', Georges are 'Doad' or 'Joardie', Malcolms 'Malkie', Normans 'Norry', Samuels 'Sammy' and Thomases 'Tammy'.

Both 'Doad' and 'Boab' become aliases for the Deity in disguised oaths such as 'Selpmaboab!' (So help me God!) and 'Doad save us!'

Commonest among the disguised oaths are 'Crivvens!' 'Jings!' and 'Jeeze!' but one hears also 'Furra love urra Wee Man!' (a reference to the Infant Jesus).

The Adversary is frequently invoked as 'Aul Nick', 'The Deevil' or 'The Deil'. A baker's dozen can be a 'deil's dizzen', and 'Whit the Deil...?' is a common expression.

Children for generations have known Hell as 'The Burnin Fire'. 'Oh here, you swore!' a little girl will tell her 'keelie' (hooligan) brother: 'You'll go tae the Burnin Fire.'

But Calvinism suffers from the law of diminishing returns and the idea of an eternity of torture does little to stem the small boy's enthusiasm for naughty words. Where else would our lady novelists get those expressions for their books?

Edward's contraction 'Ned' is used in Glasgow to denote a young tough. 'Thoan's a proaper ned', you will hear. Or 'A bunch o neds' is sometimes used instead of 'Yobos' ('boys' in back slang).

Nicknames are rife in the city streets — 'Pimple' for Dalrymple, 'Smidger' (Smith), 'Stewpot' or 'Stewrabeef' (Stewart), 'Bucky' (Buchanan), 'Jimmy' (Jamieson), 'Hammy' (Hamilton), 'Tommy' (Thomson), 'Four-Eyes' or 'Speckydoadle' (for a spectacles-wearer), 'ra Monk' or 'Puggie' (for a monkey-faced person), 'Podger', 'Kytie', 'Turkey' or 'Faa'y' (for a fat person), 'Pudden' or 'Tumshy' (for a hefty type) and 'Grumphie' (for an ill-natured one).

Girls characteristically try to change the names by which they have been known for years, as they might change the colour of their hair. It must be galling for an Isabel or an Isabella to be called 'Bell' or 'Bella' all her life, and for a Margaret, named after Malcolm Canmore's saintly queen, to be doomed to 'Maggie' or 'Meg'.

The city abounds in 'Aggies', 'Beenies', 'Teenies' and 'Feemies'.

Bernadettes and Deirdres are treated with more respect.

An aul Glasgow wife was exasperated to hear that one of her many granddaughters was to be called 'Hazel'.

She gasped: 'Selpmaboab! Aw thae lovely saints' names tae choose fae, an' they go and cry her efter a nut!'

'Spile aw da Harry-ma-Lauder records.'

From away back an important contribution to the flow of Glasgow speech has come from the many immigrant communities which have been attracted by the development of a big industrial and commercial city.

Basically Glasgow is a Lanarkshire town and its tongue is not far removed in its original form from that of Robert Burns. But in the Industrial Revolution the Celts, always there to some extent from pre-Roman times, flocked in, in greater numbers, bringing Gaelic ways of saying things from both Ireland and the Highlands.

Mickey-taking of the immigrant forms a part of all British humour and it has been strong in Glasgow since the Irish and the 'Tewchters' (as rude Lowlanders term the Gaels from the North and North-West) started to come in hungrily from their failed potato crops and their forced clearances.

Mockery of the Highlander is an old Lowland Scottish custom. You find it in the sixteenth-century poems of William Dunbar and others. Dunbar wound up his 'Dance of the Seven Deidly Sins' with (I modernise the spelling):

> 'Then cried Mahoun (Satan) for a Heelan pageant:
> Syne (then) ran a fiend to fetch MacFadyean
>   Far northward in a neuk (corner);
> Be (by the time) he the coronach (lament) had done shout
> Ersemen (Highlanders) so gathered him about
>   In Hell great room they took.
> Thae termagants (these ptarmigans), with tag and tatter,
> Full loud in Erse (Gaelic) began to clatter
>   And roop (caw) like raven and rook:
> The Devil sae deavit (so deafened) was with their yell
> That in the deepest pot of Hell
>   He smoorit (smothered) them with smoke.'

From then on Lowland Scottish writers were making fun of the 'Tewchters'. Robert Fergusson in eighteenth-century Edinburgh was imitating the peculiar way in which they spoke English or Scots, and Sir Walter Scott carried on the tradition.

Last century, Glasgow writers were perfecting the caricature of Highland speech.

The basis of it is that in Gaelic the sentences seem, to our way of looking at it, the wrong way round, and Highlanders are said to 'pit the kert afore the hoarse' (put the cart before the horse). Angus MacVicar's father always rendered it: 'I have a habit of putting the horse before the cart', and that illustrated another alleged tendency of the 'Tewchter', that in rendering things in English he gets completely mixed up.

Not so long ago you could buy a postcard in Argyle Street which purported to be a Highlander's letter home, and began: 'Dear August, Father the first...' We were asked to believe that the average Tewchter spoke almost like Stanley Unwin or James Joyce in *Finnegan's Wake*.

'I haven't seen you since long' was a mild example of Highland English. Professor W. J. Watson collected several genuine examples in a study of 'Interactions of Gaelic and English'. One of them was an advertisement heading in a Highland newspaper 'Found on Lost.'

In the days when the Highlands came right down to Dumbarton, it is alleged, a lass from north of the Line came to a toll-house on the city boundary. She asked the tollkeeper: 'Is this Glasgow?'

'Yes,' said he.

'Well,' went on the nut-brown maiden, 'is Aggie in?'

Another Highland lass on her first visit to the city had the misfortune to fall in the River Clyde. She was rescued by a friend, but excitedly recounted her adventure: 'I wass that frightened I thought I wass going to be swept into maternity, but, with the help of Proffidence and another girl from the North I haff lived to tell the tale.'

These are the sort of crazy, mixed-up things Highlanders are supposed to have said in our wonderful multi-lingual city:

'Always look to your own hand and neffer mind nobody's interests but your own! Let other bodies' interests look after themselfs!'

'You hardly effer see a soul you knew now, with aal them emigrationers going away to America.'

'Neffer mind! When wan door shuts, another wan closes.'

'I keep myself fit — I am a great beliefer in a healthy body in a healthy head. I am happy to say I haffn't a stiff body in all my choints.'

'Man, Donald, you are getting that fat, you will soon be as broad as you are narrow.'

'The annual cheneral meeting of this society in future will be held on the first Tuesday of August, unless it happens to be a Sunday.'

'I will tell you this about that same man. He is no chentleman and neither wass his mother before him.'

'Dougal, man, haff you got a light?'

'Yes, I haff got a light but it's out.'

'Hoo's yer tottie croap (potato crop) this year, Donald?'

'Oh, man, man, they're chust ferry good inteet, but ferry seldom whateffer.'

'Is this Glasgow? . . . Well, is Aggie in?'

There is a classic story about the Highlander who was boasting about his brother's ability as an artist: 'Man, he's terrific! He can take a wee stump of a pencil, about the size of your thumb's nose, and he'll draw a man there and a horse there, and you couldn't tell which wass which.'

As most Glaswegians have Highland blood, and some are only a generation away from Gaelic, they are usually telling the story against themselves or their near-relatives. A lot of the tales come also from travelling salesmen whose business has taken them into places where Gaelic was spoken.

Neil Munro, in writing his *Para Handy* tales as 'Hugh Foulis', imitated the peculiar speech, but his Highland hero usually scores in the stories. And he has given Glasgow talk at least two ever-lasting phrases: 'If Dougie wass here he would tell you', and 'It wass chust sublime!' — a favourite phrase of Alastair MacLean, the thriller writer, as I discovered when I interviewed him.

Long before Kerryman Tales and Dave Allen, Glaswegians were passing on jokes about Irish immigrants.

A favourite was of the Irish marksman at a Glasgow Fair show. There was a shooting gallery which took his fancy, with rows of clay pipes to shoot down and lovely big vases and 'wally dugs' offered as prizes. Pat shot down a couple of 'wally dugs' and a 'cheeny vase', and said with satisfaction 'I'll have wan av them clay pipes!'

Another Irishman saw a stuffed owl in a Sautmarket taxidermist's window. He walked in and asked: 'How much are you axin' for that flat-faced duck?'

'That's a night owl,' said the shopkeeper.

'I don't care if it's a week owl,' replied Pat. 'How much are you axin'?'

Either the Highlanders or the Irish gave Glasgow its 'wan' and 'yous' and 'yiz'. And many Glaswegians say 'owl' as well as 'aul' for 'old'. We tend to speak of the 'owl man', the 'owl fluh' or the 'owl wumman'. The Celtic forms are catching.

In addition, Glasgow has a lot of Irishisms of its own:

'It's the waant o ignorance that's wrang wi um.'

'Jist you mind your ain interference!'

Early this century the city and its hinterland had other invasions — by Lithuanian miners, popularly known as 'Poles', and Italian peasants, soon nicknamed 'Tallies'.

Unlike the Highlanders and the Irish, who had had some schooling in Standard English and were not so likely to speak, or attempt to speak, Lowland Scots, the Lithuanians and the Italians accepted Glaswegian as the language of the country, and developed a broken Scots which was much funnier even than broken English.

Glasgow humorists, on the stage and in the streets, were soon indulging in routines supposed to represent the way the 'Tallies' spoke Scots. It was the days when there were legal restrictions on selling certain articles late at night, and this was a source of great trouble to the immigrant shopkeeper:

'Ah jiss done shut-a ma shoap when there come "Knoack, knoack!" "Wha's-a dat?" "Iss-a Missiz Macapherson, your-a nice neebor."

'Ah undae aw-da bolts an' a bars. In she come. Aw she waant is-a boax-a match an' a caunle. Ah sell-a dem, jiss tae oblige, ye ken. She go oot an' Ah shut-a da shoap door again.

'Ah hardly goat-a time tae turn. "Knoack, knoack!" "Whaw's a dat?" Ye'll no believe — iss da blerra poalis. Sell-a da boax-a match an' a wee bit-a caunle after eight a cloack, whidgie get? Da blerra poalis!

'Aw-ra time hingin aboot oot dere when-a da shoap shut, lookin' fur trouble. Ah, but when da shoap open, whaur-a da blerra poalis?

'Bad boays come in-a ma shoap, brek-a da plate, bend-a da foark, scoot aw da peas on da flerr, poor aw da veenegar doon da gramataphone hoarn an' spile aw da Harry-ma-Lauder records. But whaur-a da blerra poalis?

'Brek-a ma hert! Whaur-a da blerra proafit?'

In 1940 the true Poles arrived in their regiments, and, like the Italians, were quick to pick up Glasgow ways of saying things.

Very soon they were going round the fruit shops asking for 'a punnae aipples' (a pound of apples) or 'twaw gidd oaranges'.

Now there is a new generation of Poles and half-Poles in the city, who are as fluent in Glescaranto as their next-door neighbours. Their names may be difficult to pronounce, but they sound like native Scots.

One old Glasgow wife soon became accustomed to her Polish neighbours, but when she had eye-trouble and went to the opticians for a test, she was given a chair opposite one of those sheets of letters chosen at random, and asked to read what she could:

'Oh, fur Goad's sake!' she told the eye specialist: '*Ah* cannae pronounce thae Polish names!'

Now it is the Pakistanis, the Indians and the Chinese who are beginning to speak Glescaranto with their own intonations.

'Bring iz some o this Poo Yong, Cherlie!' says the customer.

'Ah cannae,' says the waiter, known as 'Cherlie Chan'.

'It's oan ra menu, but.'

'Ah, but Poo-Yong — he's ma boass!'

'Ah jist gied them a bit steer wi ma stick.'

When the jail-break film, *The Big House*, starring Wallace Beery, was previewed in Glasgow, some bright Press agent conceived the notion of inviting prison officers and police to the cinema so that they could discuss with us how prison conditions in America differed from these here.

Through the Prisoners' Aid Society he had even invited some old lags along, and that was how I happened to find myself in the lift of Cranston's 'Pictur-hoose' with a professional burglar, or, as we say in Scotland, a housebreaker.

He was telling me how careless householders left their homes unguarded when on holiday.

'Ye kin easy tell whun there naebody in the hoose,' he explained to me. 'Ye keep a look-oot on the place, jist daunerin bye, like, an' ye kin pit a dry leaf in the key-hole an' if it's still there whun ye go back, ye ken thur naeb'dy there — if the leaf hiznae been disturbed, like.'

He kept looking at the newspaper sticking out of my jacket pocket. I must have looked like the stereotyped version of a journalist. He asked me:

'Whit paper are ye oan?'

'The *News*.'

His eyes lit up. 'Oh ay, the Buzzer!' he exclaimed.

The Buzzer was our greyhound racing tipster.

'Ach!' he smiled: 'The Buzzer's no sae bad. It's that beggar in anurra paper at pits us aw in the jile. (It's the one in another paper that lands us all in prison.)'

When I returned to the office I recounted this incident to the Buzzer (Johnny Allison), whom I found in the office library with our boxing writer, Elky Clark, and another famous Glasgow boxer, the lightweight, Johnny Macmillan.

'Ah'm gled ye tellt me that,' said the Buzzer. 'Ah've been feelin depressed aw day since Ah goat this letter fae a reader.'

He produced the letter, which was wrapped round a safety-razor blade. All it said was: 'Dear Buzzer, this is not for shaving.'

Punters, tipsters, old lags — it was a colourful culture newspaper work involved one in.

Editors frequently received such letters: 'Dear Sir, — If your racing double does not come up today, you will find my body floating in the George V Dock. — Your Constant Reader.'

As for old lags, and the 'screws' who looked after them, these I met when

I took celebrities round to lecture to them in Barlinnie and Saughton.

Jimmy Logan would warm them up with a joke: 'The warders are complaining that Ramensky is getting more holidays than they are.' Ramensky was a notorious jailbreaker, of Lanarkshire 'Polish' origin.

When Jimmy, sitting at the piano to entertain the prisoners, asked if there were any requests, one prisoner shouted: 'Don't fence me in!' and another 'Show me the way to go home!'

We had many dealings with the 'Glesca poalis'. Policemen then still wore their helmets, which were later discarded for the present-day caps with the diced bands. They were 'big shuge poalis' then, usually countrymen and often 'Heelanmen' or 'Tewchters' of the heavyweight class you would find wrestling, throwing the hammer or tossing the caber at Highland games.

An ex-member of the Force was the doorman at one newspaper office in which I worked. I met him one day in Sauchiehall Street and he reminisced with me on his years in the 'poalis'.

'Ah wiz oan the beat at night in the Cowcaddens,' he told me. 'Ah hud tae see that aw the pubs were safe unner loack an' key. An' aw thae publicans used tae leave a bucket (a drink) fur the boabby oan the beat. They wid leave it in a hidey-hole in the nixt close, an' as we went roon aw the shoaps an' tried the loacks we kent tae go nixt-door an' lay oor hauns oan the bucket.'

He told me another interesting story:

'Did ye ivver hear o Scoatch Jimmy, the biggest hoose-brekker in Scoa'land? Here his pictur, an' Ah'm the man that's staunin ahint um.'

He produced from his wallet his treasured photograph, taken in one of those 'aul-farran' Sauchiehall Street photographers' studios, with the clients elaborately posed in period furniture, and with castor-oil palms or aspidistras in the background.

It showed bearded Scotch Jimmy, in a frock coat and half tile hat, a seemingly respectable Victorian business-man, with a tall young policeman standing behind him, with his hand firmly on the house-breaker's shoulder.

'Whit happened,' the ex-constable explained to me, 'is Ah wiz walkin alang this verra street whan Ah cam face tae face wi Scoatch Jimmy, an' him aw toagged up like this, in his froack coat an' hauf-lum hat. Ah says tae him, "D'ye no mine me?" An' he says, "Ay, you're the beggar that pinched me."

'An' ye'll no believe this, but there an' then him an' me fixed up tae go intae the nearest photey shoap an' get oor pictur taen thegither, wi ma haun oan his shoother jiss the wey Ah nabbed him.'

One of my last jobs on the *Scottish Sunday Express* was to tour the city in a police patrol-car for the sake of the story. We had hardly left police head-

'. . . *wi ma haun oan his shoother jiss the wey Ah nabbed him.*'

quarters before the men received radio instructions to proceed to a house which was being burgled. We arrived at the ground-floor flat in a few minutes, but not quickly enough to apprehend the marauders, who had managed to escape through neighbouring 'backs' and 'dunnies' and were well away from the district.

We carried on touring the city, and at a corner of Ingram Street the car pulled up suddenly and one of the officers jumped out and made a bee-line for a boy who was carrying a 'big shuge' bundle on one shoulder. As the bobby approached him, the lad swiftly put his free hand behind his back, and there was a shower of sparks, apparently from his tail. After a short interview the officer came back to the car, laughing, and told us:

'His mother's in the oaspital an' he's takkin' hame some blankets they kerried her aff in. But the perr laddie happened tae be smokin a fag whun Ah jumped oot the caur, an' he thought Ah wiz gaun tae nab um fur smokin under-age!'

We were back on the road again, and this time we were speeding towards some police box in a rowdy quarter of the city, where 'a hostile crowd' had surrounded some beat policemen holding arrested men till the 'Black Maria' arrived.

When we reached the place, the van was already there, but there were a number of 'keelies' at bay on the pavement in front of a corner pub facing the box. As I stepped out of the patrol-car I found myself level with the middle buttons of a giant bobby. He looked like the twin of Scotch Jimmy's proud captor, tall, square-built and apparently carved out of hard wood.

'Having trouble?' I asked him.

His tough face broke into a broad grin:

'Och ay, they were the usual Deil's dizzen o neds waantin tae try sump'n oan, but Ah jist gied them a bit steer wi ma stick.'

He still had his truncheon in his King Kong fist, and I could imagine what a 'steer' (stir) with such a 'spurtle' (porridge-stick) would be like.

On another occasion a policeman of the old school, whose problem was sorting out parked vans and cars in a market area, said to me: 'It's no a poalisman they need here: it's a caveman wi a club.'

Many of Glasgow's stories about bobbies concern the big 'Heelanmen' or 'Tewchter' types, blood brothers of my heavyweight wrestling friend, John James Miller.

'Haud up!' one is remembered as saying: 'Haud up, or Ah'll belt ye in the belly wi ma baton.'

Some of them were true Gaels and spoke their own brand of English:

'Have you seen Constable Grant?' the sergeant asked a night patrol man.

'No, I haffn't seen him,' replied the constable, 'nor his lantern too!'

Another Highland bobby was asked: 'Do you think there will be rain tonight?'

'Well,' he pondered, 'maybe no — and maybe not.'

Another was credited with the phrase: 'It wass neither the one nor both.'

A frequent complaint of the police is that their sturdy efforts to put wrongdoers where they belong are not given any great support by the 'wiggies' (the judges).

One constable complained to me: 'They'll tak a *prig's* word afore *oors*.'

'Prig' (an old word for a thief) is still much in currency in police circles. That and 'neds' are probably the commonest words among them for the criminal fraternity.

I had an amusing experience with the 'Ruglen poalis' — the Larnarkshire police stationed in Rutherglen — when rifles were being handed out to our Home Guard company in 1940. We had to queue for them at the back door of the police station in the royal burgh's Queen Street.

There were two ministers in my platoon. One of them, the parish minister, turned up for the occasion in an ordinary collar and tie. The other, the Rev. William Wright of Wardlawhill, had just been to a funeral and was in his blacks and wearing a clerical collar.

The rifles, old American ones thick with grease, which we were to have to clean thoroughly, were handed out, one to each Local Defence Volunteer, by a hefty sergeant standing on the outside stair at the back of the 'poalis oaffice'.

We used to say the Lanarkshire police were so tall they could stand on the Main Street pavement and shift the hands of the Town Hall clock.

When the minister of the parish church stepped forward in his off-duty collar and tie, the big policeman handed him a rifle without a murmur. But when Wullie Wright followed, wearing his dog-collar, the sergeant drew back his rifle and barked: 'Naw, you're no getting yin: *it's agane the Geneva Coanvention.*'

There were rumours at that time of German paratroops landing in France dressed as priests and nuns.

Wullie accepted the sergeant's decision in good grace, went home, changed into a lounge suit and collar and tie, and came right back for his rifle.

'Ah hae tae knoack Aff tae mak room for the scuddies.'

Sir Harry Lauder never sang anything sexier than 'I Love a Lassie', 'Roamin in the Gloamin' and 'Stop Yer Ticklin, Jock'. Glasgow comics did not always keep up the tradition that Scotch comedians were clean.

Lex McLean gloried in the nickname of 'Sexy Lexy'. Yet most of the time he was 'serr hauden doon wi the muckle bubblyjoak' (sorely held down by the big turkey-cock), and in his case the 'bubblyjoak' was the Lord Chamberlain.

Much of his skill was diverted to getting away with it, and in this he had two great aids — miming (with the audience supplying the words to his dumb-show) and the Glasgow tongue. The Lord Chamberlain's Department did not seem to employ an interpreter.

One of Lex's favourite words was 'scuddies' — meaning nudes. He told the story of two simple country chaps walking along a lane and coming to a high wall surrounding a nudist colony. The first climbed up and shouted down to his 'china': 'Here scuddies!' (Here are some naked people.)

'Are they men or weemin?' asked the lad below.

'Ah cannae tell,' said the one looking over the wall: 'They've nae claes oan.'

One show, in which I saw Lex, was being followed by a late-night nude show. It was the time when such shows were fashionable, and threatening the death of British variety.

Lex signed off with 'Noo Ah hae tae knoack aff tae mak room fur the scuddies.'

He was using a Glasgow contraction of the Scots word 'scuddie-nakit', meaning stark-naked. In his stories, 'in the scud' meant in the nude.

Another of his favourite words was 'shuch'. This is the West of Scotland way of saying 'sheuch', the Scots word for a ditch. Lex used it to mean muck. 'In the shuch', to him, meant up to the neck in it.

A typical story told by Lex was of the man who went on to a railway train and discovered 'his bits wiz aw shuch' (his boots were all covered with muck). As the train started, he sat down and wiped his boots with a newspaper, which he threw out of the window.

As luck would have it, the man in the next compartment was looking out of the window at the time and he got the newspaper and its contents full in the face. He ran into the corridor and into the offender's compartment, yelling: 'Whit the bleezes are ye playin at?

'Ah could ask *you* that,' replied the other, laughing: 'Tak a look at yer

Glasgow comics have always been natural speakers of the racy local tongue.

face! It's aw shuch!' (It's covered with muck.)

Billy Connolly has followed in this bold tradition, and Billy is luckier than Lex, with the Lord Chamberlain no longer vetting scripts. Billy is, as Scots say, 'aye there or there-aboot' — undermining our pretence to be douce Presbyterians who do not laugh at 'shuch'.

Whatever our pretence is, the general assumption about the cultural and artistic tastes of the Scots is that they have a strong sense of gravity — in the sense of being low on the ground, rather than serious.

Listening to my transistor recently, I heard Haig Gordon, in 'Good Morning, Scotland!', on the BBC asking an interviewee: 'After all, isn't the average Scotsman's idea of entertainment a cup of hot beef tea and a meat pie?' A bit hard, considering the Embruh Festival, nat.

Glasgow comics have always been natural speakers of the racy local tongue, and they have used it in their acts, while having to dilute it, lest strangers should fail to understand them. They have all been famous for their typically Glesca catch-phrases.

Tommy Morgan, the big 'baw-faced' favourite of the Pavilion audiences, used 'Clerty, Clerty!' — his mother's way of saying 'I declare to goodness!' — equivalent to the American mothers' 'Well, I declare!'

Another of Tommy's local phrases was 'Ah'm noany play', a small boy's way of saying: 'I'm not going to play.' It is typical of the Glaswegian's manner of running words together.

Jack Anthony's catch-phrase, which he used ever after it won an unsought-for laugh in one of his sketches, was 'Nae bawther at aw' — No trouble at all. With his good stage diction, he said it more distinctly than some of his townies, who would pronounce it 'Naeborrataw'. Jack used it sarcastically towards someone who was asking too much.

The great comic star of the Twenties and Thirties, Tommy Lorne, a 'skinnymalinky long-legs, wi umberella feet' and a clown's face and shock of hair, made play with 'soassitches' (sausages) and pies — there was a small-boy touch about his natural humour. 'Ah'm pashnitly foan (passionately fond),' he would say in his high-pitched cracked voice, 'o a cuppla soassitches fur ma brekfist oan a Sunday moarin.' Nothing very funny about this in the script, but to hear him solemnly declare his passion, with his long-fingered white gloves twittering at his lips, could shake the whole theatre.

He referred frequently to 'the aul wife in the pie-shoap at Lumphannans'. Why this was funny would baffle Darwin or Freud to explain; it not only won a laugh each time it was said, but it left the audience with an aching void if he omitted to mention it.

Scotch comics got so many laughs, with such 'hamely' asides, that an

English comedian I knew well and liked, Stainless Stephen, swore they had only to show their tartan trews and say 'Och ay!' to raise a laugh with a Glasgow audience. Yet these audiences are reputed to be the toughest in the world, and Glasgow Empire was credited with being 'the graveyard of English comedians'.

Sausages came into the small-boy act of Jimmy Logan, the brilliant scion of the Short, or Logan, family which included Ma and Pa Logan of the Metropole; Ella Logan, the Broadway jazz singer, and Annie Ross, Jimmy's jazz-singing sister. Jimmy's catch-phrase in his early days was 'Soassitches is the boays!'

There was a time when West End, Panloaf Glaswegians went 'slumming' for laughs — to the Princess Theatre in the Gorbals and the Queen's near Glasgow Cross. George West in the Princess pantomimes carried Christmas into early summer with his 'Haw Wull!' humour.

George's shows were clean, but 'shuch' was a commodity at the Queen's. Mainly, however, it was a friendly, neighbourhood theatre where the principal comedian, Sam Murray, greeted the audience with 'Hullaw, chinas!' It was his use of this word which kept it in currency long after rhyming slang had passed its heyday.

The other stars there were Frank and Doris Droy, who were later a popular club act in England.

I took part with Doris in a radio feature along with my journalistic colleague, Jack House, and a young Jimmy Logan. I found Doris a douce Glasgow housewife interested in her knitting and quite different from her sensational stage character of 'Suicide Sal', cast in the pantomime programme as 'Fanny Cartwright'.

Doris was an expert in Glescaranto, and also an inspired performer who made us laugh with the sheer ingenuousness of her act. She was just naturally 'ra life an' sowl urra perty'.

If she got a laugh for a gag, she would say, like a wee lassie: 'Didgie fancy that? Ah goat it oot wanny ma Christmas crackers.' (I got it out of one of my Christmas crackers.)

Some Christmas crackers!

Other acts at the Queen's would dance with their stockingless feet thrust into unlaced Army boots, which gave the taps more of a clatter, and would even play the comb-and-paper and the 'spins' (spoons rattled up and down the legs, palms, arms and body) like buskers.

The piano needed tuning. 'Ye get a better soon oot it that wey,' I was told.

The 'soon' (sound) of that jangling piano was the true 'soon' of Glasgow.

In Candleriggs, at least twice a day, for years, I passed the same man.

Candleriggs was the home of the fruit market and he was something in that line. Every time he passed he said the same thing in that musical Glasgow voice: 'Hullawrerr!' (Hullo, there!)

This warm caressing phrase was adopted by Rikki Fulton in his role as Josie in the 'Francie and Josie' series with Jack Milroy, another expert in the local speech.

Catch-phrases were used by all the old comics, and they were always adopted from the way ordinary Glasgow folk speak.

Lauder's was 'Noo mine Ah'm tellin ye!' (Now remember I'm telling you!) His contemporary, Neil Kenyon, had the phrase: 'Izzat a fack?' (Is that a fact?) and eventually he worked it into a song: 'I walked away and said: "Is that a fact?"'

Some of the most successful Scotch comedians — Johnny Beattie and Chick Murray, for instance — use plain English practically all the time, which makes their very rare use of Scots all the funnier when it occurs.

Stanley Baxter has patented the treatment of Glescaranto as a subject for mock-serious language studies in his 'Parliamo Glasgow' series, and in it has probably devised the most brilliant stage method of putting the vernacular across to those who do not speak it or meet it in daily life. At the same time he gives Glaswegians themselves a 'knowing' laugh.

In fact, however, Glasgow comics have been doing this for years, though not in such polished style. The experts at it in my early years of theatre-going, before and during the Great War of 1914-18, were a couple called Lindsay and Hart — Bret Hart and Dora Lindsay.

Hart played the Panloaf feed who affected to be bewildered by Dora's Gallowgate expressions. He would be the manager of a shoe shop, and she would come in, wearing a shawl (it was the days when Glasgow still had its shawled women known as 'shawly wifes', or simply 'shawlies'), and leading a child by the hand, and demand: 'Seez a perra bits fur meena wane!' (Give me a pair of boots for me and the child!)

'Seize?' Hart echoed, stupidly, making the gesture of seizing something. Dora went through the same rigmarole again and it took the whole act for Hart to tumble to the fact that what she wanted was, in fact, two separate pairs of shoes for herself and the child.

The clash of Panloaf and Glescaranto is still good for a laugh, for most of us have had real-life experience of it, though most Glaswegians will politely speak English to strangers, whatever they normally speak to their 'chinas'.

Most incomprehensible are the hordes who descend on London for the 'fitbaw' battle between 'weers' (our side) and the 'Aul Enemy' (England), those 'wee fluhs' who have been described as 'aw tammies (all Tam o' Shanter bonnets) an' nae teeth'. The 'wallies' are left at 'hame' for safety.

'Ye're aye sherry a rerr terr at ra Ferr.'

Glasgow's social calendar begins on New Year's Day, known locally as 'Nerrday'. The same word is applied to the drink one is given to celebrate the coming of the New Year.

'Huv ye hud yer Nerrday yit?'

We have scarcely got over the prolonged period of exchanging Nerrdays before we are into the Burns season. Our National Bard had the foresight to be born on January 25, which brings him well into the natural season·for celebration.

Not all Burns associations in Glasgow go in for heavy potations. One of them, the Scottish Burns Club, is teetotal. I was at another, in Uddingston, where the working-class participants brought their families along and were accordingly sober, though not totally abstemious.

This was the dinner at which I was presented with a church-warden pipe, a tradition of the society. I was told: 'If ye manage tae get that hame tae Ruglen withoot brekkin it, ye muss be sober.'

I managed it.

Just like the spirit of Nerrday, the spirit of pantomime in Glasgow extends well into the year. And local clubs and societies use every opportunity to keep up celebrations on dates of their own, including block bookings at the pantomime.

Pantomime comics make a feature of greetings from the stage to the members of these organisations, having been postcarded in advance, and 'a gidd time is hud be aw'.

One of the early festivals for the children is April the First which in most parts of Scotland is known as 'Hunt-the-gowk' (Hunt-the-cuckoo) Day, but in Glasgow has become Magowk. Where other Scots children may jeer, after taking someone in, ' 'Sa Huntygowk,' your Glaswegians say more succinctly, 'Magowk!' (My cuckoo, or my fool.)

Somebody who has been taken in by a confidence trick, or believed something that was flagrantly not true, will be asked, in adult circles: 'Wha gied ye a magowk?'

After all the excuses for celebration which make the long winter more bearable have been exhausted, Glasgow looks forward to the joys of spring and summer and especially to the annual holiday fortnight known as the Ferr.

'Ye're aye sherry a rerr terr at ra Ferr,' they say optimistically (You are always sure of an exceptionally good time at Glasgow Fair.)

Some of them make sure of a good send-off to the holiday by getting 'puggelt' on Ferr Friday, which is a kind of mid-year Hugmunay.

Traditionally the Ferr was the occasion for Paw, Maw and the wanes to flock to the seaside with spades and pails, Paw looking forward to wading in the sea with his trousers rolled above his knees while the wanes built their sand-castles. Paw showed off his ability to 'oar' a boat and Maw did a 'Knees up, Mother Brown' act, dancing barelegged in the tide.

Their targets were the familiar seaside resorts — Millport in the island of Muckle Cumbrae, Rothesay (affectionately known as 'Rossie') in the Isle of Bute and Dunoon in the Argyll reach called Cowal. Cowal's also were among the most important Highland Games and Highland Gatherings.

Nowadays Paw, Maw and the wanes tend to go much farther afield even than Campbeltown, the Isle of Man, Portobello, the Highlands and North of Scotland and over the water to Ireland. Costa Brava, Ibiza, the Black Forest, Vienna, wherever the travel agents' posters beckon from — and there are 'thoosans' of travel agents in Glasgow — the modern Glaswegians will go.

Yet the faithful still swear by 'Sweet Rossie Bay', 'Doon at Dunoon', and Burntisland in Fife, places with which their Grampaws were familiar. 'Doon the Watter' (sailing down the Clyde or taking the train to its resorts, including Ayr and Prestwick and Troon, Ardrossan and Saltcoats) still has its appeal.

Pantomime comics at this season become seaside entertainers with their landlady jokes, such as Johnny Beattie's routine: 'I asked her for an alarm clock and she said, "Ye dinnae need an alarm clock, ye'll hear me scrapin the toast in the moarnin." We knew we were getting roly-poly puddin when we saw her wi wan stocking on.'

Glaswegians who go abroad often look for the same delights as they would experience at Rossie and Dunoon. 'See thae Tallies (Italians)? They mak faur better fish suppers in Glesca nor whit they dae in their ain country, an' at's as fack's daith.'

'Noo Ah wunner whit wey that is?'

'Ah dinnae ken. Mebbe it needs the Glesca err (air), but.'

Holiday-making, Glasgow-style, is exhausting, and they are all secretly glad to get back to home conditions; as they put it, 'back tae aul claes an'. purritch' (back to old clothes and porridge).

The children are usually glad to get back to 'the skill' (the school), where there is companionship to offset the tedium of 'gettin learnt'.

Landladies may complain of the short season, the fact that our summer starts late and closes early (though for a brief spell we boast longer days than in the South, and some years we have really glorious summers, especially on Clydeside and even in the North), but on the whole we are a race conditioned to accommodating ourselves to the long winter.

Robert Burns's poetry is largely about the fun of living in Scotland in winter. We have a saying, 'We nivver deed a winter yit.' (We never died in any winter so far.) Another of our sayings is 'A green Yule maks a fat kirkyaird', in other words, frost and snow are good for you. Perhaps the saying was invented by curlers, who have been known to complain: 'Sax open winters in a raw' (Six winters in succession without ice — a terrible calamity if you like bonspiels).

Winter festivals come close on the heels of summer. Halloween is popular with Glasgow children, not only for the fun of 'dookin fur aipples' (ducking in a tub or 'washin-byne' for apples and nuts) but also for the opportunity to go guising.

'Guisers' were rather like the English Christmas waits and used to do a bit of real entertaining for their pennies. Now in Glasgow they tend to be youngsters with their clothes on inside out and their faces blackened, saying little beyond 'Please tae help the guisers!' strangely like the Cockney kids' wail of 'Help the guy, sir!'

How many of them still sing—

'Ah took her tae a ball,
  Ah took her tae her supper,
She fell owre a cherr
  An' stuck her nose in ra butter.
Ra butter, ra butter,
  Ra holy-marjarine (oleo-margarine)—
Two black eyes an' a jeely nose
  An' a face aw pentit green'?

Halloween and Hogmanay guisers had a repertory of songs in the old days along with a masquerade called 'Galoshans', whose name is said to be a corruption of the Epistle to the Galatians.

But still the Halloween parties do something to keep alive the party pieces — rhymes, recitations and songs:

'Kiltie, Kiltie Calder
  Couldnae play a drum—
His faither took the bellusiz (bellows)
  An' blew um up the lum.' (Up the chimney.)

Tam, Tam, the funny wee man
Washed his face in the fryin-pan,
Combed his herr wi the leg o a cherr,

Tam, Tam the funny wee man.'

Hi diddle dandy,
Black sugar candy,
Gie yer wanes whit ye like
But dinnae gie them brandy!'

'Hi Joack ma cuddie!
Ma cuddie's oan the dyke,
An' if ye touch ma cuddie,
Ma cuddie 'ull gie ye a bite—
          Hooch!'

Young or old, winter is definitely the time to enjoy yourself in Glasgow.

'That pirn stuck wi preens on Gilmorehill.'

Sometimes Glasgow, contemplating the changes and nostalgic for the past (perhaps a past that never was), calls itself the Sickened City. Old-timers complain that they could get lost in their native 'toon'.

'Whit wi aw thae flee-owres and jook-unners an' spaghetti junctions, it's no the same place at aw. Whaur's Croon Street, whaur's the Spootmooth, whaur's awra places we yist tae ken? Whaur's the Goose Dubs? D'ye ken this? If a motorist stoapped an' axed me, Ah couldnae direck him tae oany o thae places. Ah might fin ma wey tae them on fit (on foot), but Ah'm damned if Ah'd ivver ken hoo ye could get there in a caur.'

It was so much simpler when you could say: 'Green caurs go east', when the electric trams had colours as well as destination boards to guide the would-be traveller.

Although of course there was the conductress who had forgotten to change her boards and someone asked: 'Whaur's this caur supposed tae be gaun?'

'Whidgie mean "supposed tae be gaun"? This caur's definitely gaun tae Auchenshuggle, an' nae "supposed tae' aboot it. Can ye no read whit it says oan the front?'

'Ay, Ah kin read, hen, but maybe you cannae. It says "Auchenshuggle" oan the front awright, but it says "Paisley" oan the side.'

'Lissen, Smertie!' retorted the conductress. 'This caur goes front-weys, no sidey-weys.'

The changes in the town are like the changes in society and the economy; it is the older ones who feel them. The young take the city, the social system and the economy, as of now, whether they approve or not, but the 'aul yins', or the 'owl wans', dream of the days they knew:

'Awb'dy (everybody) kens whit the bawther is noo: owre munny hauns yucky (too many hands itchy) fur merr siller (more money). Even the berns are at it. Naeb'dy seems tae hae the sense tae see at, the merr we get, the dearer awthing bid tae be, an' sae we'll nivver get oot the bit. We were haurd din tae and haurd up, Goad kens, in the aul days, but perr as we aw were, we could aye mak a fen (fend for ourselves). At's the bawther we them aw the-day: nane o them can cope.'

Someone recalled that in the handloom weaving days on Clydeside you could tell how well (or badly) the weavers were being fed, by the rhythm of the shuttle:

'If the weavers wiz oan shoart rations, the shuttle droned awaw: "Hauf a herrin an' hauf a bannock." If there wiz some improvement ye heard it singin a wee bit slicker tune — "A herrin an' a bannock, a herrin an' a bannock.'" If things goat better still it went: "A herrin an' a hauf an' a bannock an' a hauf." But coandeetions hud tae be rael gidd tae speed it up tae "Twaw herrin twaw bannocks twaw herrin twaw bannocks."' '

Despite all the changes Glasgow preserves a lot of its Victoriana. It was Dr Tom Honeyman, physician, art dealer, amusing orator and eventually the city's art director, who characterised the spire of the University as 'that pirn stuck wi preens (that bobbin stuck with pins) on Gilmorehill', as typical of the over-elaboration of some of the Victorian buildings — happy hunting grounds for the 'doos' and 'stuckies'.

Now new blocks appear and old blocks are either pulled down or cleaned up and renovated. Rain and 'stoory' (fierce and dusty) winds gave the city a dirty face, rain ranging from a mere smirr as we call it, to 'ferr spittin' or a 'thunnerplump, a rael doon-poor'.

'It wiz rainin cats an' dugs an' Ah couldnae get oan fur jookin the poodles (dodging the puddles)', one of our old comics used to crack.

The weather lined the ponderous Victorian buildings with a century of 'sit' (soot) or 'coom', and from the 'rones', ledges and 'whigmaleeries an' purlicues' and other ornamentation beloved of Betjeman, the 'doos' and the 'stuckies' sent down their streams of 'pen' to streak the stone with action painting.

Yet 'aul Mungo's' sixth-century 'dear green place' beside the Molendinar burn still contrives to smile verdantly through the 'dreich' (drab) colouring, with parks and riverside walkways, much improved in recent years — for instance at Custom House Quay.

Whether the city is the attraction or the subtle quality of its people, Glasgow has a strong hold on the affection of its citizens and all who have ever dwelt there, and now it is more and more exercising its appeal on the visitor from other parts of Scotland and further afield. It is becoming the Mecca of the discerning tourist, along with its panorama of delights — the Clyde.

Glasgow poets said it all long ago. Blin Alec (Alexander McDonald), McGonagall's only rival, used to recite to passers-by in the Trongate:

> 'Ah've travelled the whole world over
> And many a place beside,
> But Ah nivver did see a more beautifuller city
> Than that on the banks of the navigatable river,
> the Clyde.'

And Patrick Buchanan sang to the holidaymakers at the Ferr:

> 'Ah hud a hat, Ah hud nae merr,
> Ah goat it frae the hatter.
> Ma hat wiz smashed, ma skull laid berr,
> Yae nicht whun oan the batter.

> 'An' noo tae see us packed an' crammed
> Like oany Yankee squatter,
> Nae less than five in ilka bed—
> That's high life doon the watter.'

Glasgow's aura — Aura Boays, Aura Girra, Aura Best

Standard Scots has evolved its spelling over the centuries but the printed word in our national literature does not convey how these words are pronounced in Glasgow, For instance, 'perr' (poor) is spelt *puir*, 'abin' (above) is spelt *abune*. Some Glasgow poets — notably Stephen Mulrine and Tom Leonard — write the Glasgow dialect as it really sounds. This glossary of everyday Glasgow terms is spelt phonetically.

ABETTOR	An urge: 'Abettor get crackin.'
ABIN	Above: 'Glesca's abin thum aw.'
ABLOW	Opposite of 'abin': 'He's ablow contemp.'
AFF	On the turn: 'At's a bit aff, Mac.'
AFORE	Formerly: 'Afore ye cam up, Jimmy.'
AGANE	Opposed to: 'The minister preached oan adultery — he seemed tae be agane it.'
AHEID	In the future: 'Ye nivver ken whit's aheid o yiz.'
AHIN	Behind; supporting: 'Ye need some money ahin ye.'
ALANG	Along: 'Ah like minsh alang wi ma totties.'
ALLOO	Permit: 'Here, you, that's no allooed.'
ALOWE	On fire: 'It wiz owre damp tae set alowe.'
AMANG	Among: 'Thur no a rael man amang ra lotty yiz.'
ARRA	Arrow: are the: 'We arra people.'
AT	That; who; which.
AURA	The friendly atmosphere of Glasgow: Aura Boays, Aura Girra, Aura Latest Results, Aura Winners, Aura Same, Aura Best!
AWAW	Away; also, a wall.
AWTHEGITHER	Posh way of saying 'Aura Girra.'
BACK	Space at back of tenements.
BAGS	Plenty, often 'Bagsa plenny' or 'Plenny bags.'
BATTER	Booze: 'He's oan ra batter again.'
BAMSTICK	Useless person, dead loss, stumer.
BAP	Breakfast roll, foot: 'Gie yer baps a rest!'
BAPFITTIT	Flatfooted.
BASHUM	'Hit him!'
BAWHEID	Stupid person.

BELDYHEIDIT	Bald; reckless: 'He went beldyheidit at it.'
BEN	Inside: 'Come ben and mak yersel at hame!'
BENDER	Booze-up.
BEVVY	Quantity of beverage.
BIGHEID	Conceited person.
BINT	Girl.
BIRL	Whirl, waltz: 'Fancy a birl oan ra flerr, like?'
BLAW	Blow, boast, boaster: 'See him? He's jiss a blaw.'
BIZARRE	Store basement with a Santa Claus.
BOAK	Sick turn: 'Her singin gies me ra boaks.'
BOASS	Employer.
BOAY	Boy, buoy, member of San Toy.
BREW	Make tea; Social Security bureau.
BRURRA	Brother.
BRITHER	Same as brurra.
CAESAR	Command: 'Caesar read urra racin!'
CAKEY	Kooky: 'They were a character we cawed Cakey Annie.'
CAMPHOR	Purpose: 'At's whit Ah camphor.'
CAW	Call, name, drive: 'Caw ra wringer fur me, coack.'
CHANCER	Con-man.
CHANTY-WRASSLER	A contemptible person.
CLART	Dirt.
CLARTY	Dirty.
CLAW	Scratch, buzz off! 'Awaw'n claw!'
CLED	Clothed, full up.
CLEG	Gadfly.
CLERTY	I declare to...!
CLESS	Class.
CLOOR	Smite, lump from blow: 'Ah'll cloor ye.'
CLOSE	Entry to stair.
COOKIE	Sweet bun.
COORDIE	Coward.
CRACK	Conversation: 'Come ben an' gie's yer crack!'
CRAP	Throw in the towel, capitulate.
CRAW	Crow.
CUPPLA	Two.
DANNYLION	Dandelion; traffic warden.
DAUD	Lump, piece: 'Slip in a daud o cheese, hen!'

DAUDLE	Easy job, walkover.
DAUR	Dare: 'Ah daur ye.' 'Ay, a daursay.'
DEEF	Deaf: 'He's as deef's a door-nail.'
DICK	Detective.
DID	Done: 'See whit ye've went and did!'
DIN	Done, did.
DIZ	Does.
DIZNAE	Does not.
DOAKEN	Dock-leaf, nothing: 'Ah dinnae gie a doaken.'
DOLL	Ma'am: 'Yur awaw pass yer stoap, doll.'
DONE	Did: 'He ferr done his nut, so he did.'
DOOK	Duck, swim: 'It wiz owre caul fur a dook.'
DOWP	Backside, fag-end.
DRAP	Drop, a drink, sometimes 'drappie.'
DREEP	Drip, drop down a wall.
DRIECH	Drab, dreary (of weather or a sermon).
DROOK	Soak.
DRUCKEN	Intemperate.
DUMP, DUNT	A blow: 'Ah'll gie ye a dump oan ra broo.'
EN	End.
ERR	Ayr, air, there: 'Err a cherr owre err.'
ET	Ate, eaten: 'Ah've ett yer piece.'
EX	Axe.
FAITHER	Father.
FANKLE	Tangle: 'Ye've goat yer galluses in a fankle.'
FARRA	Same as faither.
FAWN	Fallen.
FEART	Afraid: 'Thur nu-hin tae be feart fur.'
FEBBERWURRY	February.
FELL	Fallen: 'Ah've went an' fell in love again.'
FERR	Fare, fair, Glasgow Fair.
FIN	Find, feel: 'Ah hink Ah fin a smell o gas.'
FITBAW	Football.
FLEG	Frighten.
FLERR	Flair, flare, floor: 'Seeza sherra ra flerr!'
FLET	Flat, saucer: 'A single-en oan ra toap flet.'
FLIT	Remove house — used even when the rent is paid.
FOO	Full, drunk: 'As foo as a puggie.'
FOOSTY	Mouldy: 'A wee foosty Jenny Awthing's.'

FUN	Found, felt, smelt: 'Ah fun the awfiest smell.'
FURTIVE	To have: 'He muss be aul furtive saw sae much.'
GALLUS	Devil-may-care: 'Ah like a lass tae be gallus.'
GAMMY	Lame: 'He hud a gammy leg.'
GANDER	Look: 'Tak a gander at thae bizzies!'
GAUN	Going: 'Ah've loast a gidd-gaun umberella.'
GAWKY	Gauche: 'He hud a gey gawky luck oan his face.'
GEEZER	Give me a: 'Geezer read urra results!'
GEY	Rather, very: 'He's gey fly, that yin.'
GLAUR	Muck: 'Ah fan masel up tae ra oaxters in glaur.'
GLED	Happy: 'Come ben! Ah'm gled tae see ye!'
GLEG	Smart: 'He's no verra gleg in the uptak.'
GLERR	Glare: 'Whit ye glerrin at, Jimmy?'
GOAT	Got: 'Ah din owre much wark fur whit Ah goat.'
GRAMP	Short for Grampaw, grand-dad.
GRAMMAR	Grandmother.
GRAUN	Grand: 'We hud a graun feed o thoan choaped Shooey.'
GRUN	Terra firma: 'Ah you'll get, Jimmy, is six feeta grun.'
HAEN	Had: 'Ah shoulda haen merr'n Ah haen at the feenish.'
HAMAHADDY	Excuse, alibi: 'Ay, it's a fine hamahaddy.'
HAPNY	Halfpenny: 'Ah gien um ma last hapny.'
HARD MAN	Crook, heavy: 'He kerries oan like a hard man.'
HAVER	Talk nonsense: 'It wiz jiss a loata havers.'
HEELANMAN'S UMBRELLA	Bridge over Argyle Street sheltering Gaelic speakers, Poles, Pakistanis and those who talk the deaf-and-dumb language, when they want to meet their group for a rain-free talk.
HEID	Head: 'Ah gien um wan wirra heid an' twaw wirra bunnet.'
HEN	Term of endearment; 'Ma'am!': 'Ye'll hae tae pey furra dug, hen.'
HINK	Think: 'Whidgie hink urra talent?'
HING	Hang: 'Ah like a gidd hing owra windae.'
HIZNAE	Has not: 'He hiznae a cat in hell's chance.'
HOARSE	Horse: 'He's that hoarse he muss drink oot a troch.'
HOAST	Cough: 'At's a serr smoker's hoast ye've goat.'

HOCHS	Legs: 'She hiznae much o a face but she's goat a graun perra hochs.'
HUD	Hold: 'Huddiz!' might mean 'haddocks' or 'Hold me!'
HUGMUNAY	New Year's Eve: 'Rise up and geeze wur Hugmunay!'
HURSEL	Herself: 'She hiz a tip aboot hursel, that yin.'
HUT	Hit: 'Ah haurly luckt at um an' he hut me wan.'
HUVNAE	Have not: 'Soarry, Mac, Ah huvnae a clue.'
JAICKET	Jacket: 'Ah like totties bilet in thur jaickets.'
JALOOZE	Suspect: 'The bizzies jaloozed we were up tae tricks.'
JAM	Good luck: 'Yer jam's in, Jimmy.'
JAUP	Splash: Tommy Morgan joked 'The tanks oot east hiz special mudgairds fur tae keep the Jaups aff.'
JAWBOAX	Sink, and the jawhole is the drain.
JENNY WILLOCKS	Hermaphrodite.
JESSIE	An effeminate man: 'Awaw, ya big Jessie!'
JILE	Jail, imprison: 'Fines are nae gidd, Ah'd jile the loat.'
JINKIES	A question: 'Jinkies wan o them?'
JIMMY	Sir! Secretly it means: 'Ya toffee-nosed get!'
JINGS	Dear, dear! *Mon Dieu!*
JOAB	One's employment.
JOATTERS	The sack: 'Dae yer joab or ye'll get yer joatters.'
JUCK	A duck: 'He wauchles aboot like a shilliefittit juck.'
KAIL	Soup, made with kail or cabbage.
KEN	Know: ''S no whit ye ken, 's whaw ye ken.' (It's not what you know, but whom.)
KEP	Catch, kept, delayed: 'Whit kep ye?'
KERR	Care: 'If ye kerred fur me ye widnae kerry oan.'
KERRYOOTS	Takeaway meals or drinks: 'He's loadit wi kerryoots.'
KERT	Cart, carry off: 'Ah'll no leave this hoose till Ah'm kertit.'
KNEW	Known: 'If Ah hudduv knew, Ah widnae been there.'
LASS	Girl, lass: 'Shur lass chance, lass!'

LAW	Trouble, as in Murn Law; not so bad, in Farn Law and Brurn Law, and Cistern Law may even be fun.
LEA	Leave: 'Kin ye no lea'z alane?'
LEAMALANE	Let him alone.
LEARN	Teach: 'Wan hing: they learnt us gidd English there.'
LEE	Tell lies: 'Ye lee, ye lee, ye leear lood' (old ballad).
LEEAR	One who lies: 'Ye'd mak me oot a leear.'
LEN	Loan, lend: 'Seeze a len o yer spunks, Mac!'
LEP	Leapt, also 'lowped' or 'lowpit'.
LEST	Stay the distance: 'He lestit oot tae the lass lap.'
LIT	Allow, let: 'Lit um alane, Ah tell ye!'
LUCK	Look; inspect: 'He's needin his heid luckt.'
LUG	Ear: 'It's a skelp'n the lug you're waantin.'
LUM	Chimney: 'He still believes Santy comes doon ra lum.'
LUP	Impudence: 'An' Ah'll hae nae merr o yer lup, see?'
MA	My.
MAN	Husband: 'You're lucky ye've still goat yer man.'
MAP	Face: 'Ma man cam hame wi ''Gers wan'' aw owre his map.'
MAW	Mother: 'Geeze a piece, Maw!'
MEN	Repair.
MESSAGES	Errands, shopping.
MERIT	Married; additional: 'Whit's merit's a diaboalical liberty.'
MERR	More: 'The merr the merrier.'
MERRY	Mary: 'Ah'm gonny merry Merry.'
MERRYHILL	Maryhill.
MEY	May, month or girl's name.
MIN	Moon: 'He cam hame wi a face like a foo min.'
MINE	Quarry for ideas and memories: 'D'ye no mine me?' 'Smashed oties mine.' (Mid-Atlantic for 'foo as a puggie.')
MINSH	Beef, 'carried off in a state of collops.'
NAE	No: 'Huv ye nae sense, man?'
NAEB'DY	Nobody. 'Naeb'dy loves me.'
NANE	None: 'Ah nivver goat nane.'

NAT	And that; et cetera.
NEB	Nose; nark: 'Awright if she widnae keep nebbin at me.'
NEEPS	Turnips: 'Haggis, champit totties an' bashed neeps.'
NED	A young crook: 'He's a proaper ned, that yin.'
NEIGHBOUR	No trouble: 'Neighbour ataw, Mac!'
NELLY	Lifetime: 'Nut oan yer Nelly.'
NERRA	Narrow: 'It's as nerra's a spunk' (as narrow as a match).
NERRDAY	New Year's Day: 'Ye huvnae gien me na Nerrday yit.'
NICK	Lock-up: 'The nick? You're lucky — Ah góat hame!'
NIP	Small whisky, it gets smaller every year.
NO	Not: 'This is no ma ain hoose.'
NOAD	Credit: 'Ah goat it oan the noad.'
NOAK	Clock: 'Ma man fergoat tae wine the noak.'
NOO	Now: 'Noony-noony, at's no the road, noo!'
NUH-HIN	Nothing: 'Ah nivver goat nuh-hin fur ma pains.'
NUT	Not (emphatic): 'Nut a tall, nut a tall!'
OOR	Our, same as wur; also hour: 'It'll tak hauf-an-oor.'
OOT	Out, out of: 'She taen a notion tae eat putty an' aw her windaes fell oot.'
OOTBYE	Outside.
PAA'ER	Patter; also, swank: 'Ye should see the paa'er!'
PAW	Father: 'Poo Paw poo!' (Phrase in 'Oarin raboa'.)
PED	'Athaleet' who takes part in foot races.
PEEVER	Hopscotch: 'Awa'n play wi yer peever!'
PERR	Poor. 'The perrs-hoose' was the poorhouse.
PLERR	Footballer: 'The neds jiss coapy the plerrs.'
POKE	Bag; goal.
POO	Pull: 'Ah'm waitin oan Ernie tae poo ma number oot the poke.'
POOR	Pour: 'It's poorin weet.' 'Rotten merridge: nae poor-oot.'
POWE	Head of hair, skull: 'She gien um a bowel-croap aw roon his powe.'
PRERR	Prayer: 'He upset awbody, like a dug at a prerr meetin.'

PRESS	Cupboard: 'She's goat as much in the press as Maggie Thatcher.
PRIG	Thief, crook. 'It taks a prig tae catch a prig.'
PUGGIE	Monkey, also temper: 'Ah hink this driver's goat his puggie up.' 'Whitivver Ah said, she leff in a puggie.'
PUNNA, Punny	Pound of. (Weight only.)
RA	The great god Ra of the Glasgow comics: the.
RABOA	Comics' spelling for 'the boat'.
RACCOON	A stupid fellow: 'Raccoon's needin his heid luckt.'
RAMORRA	Tomorrow.
RAPPORT	Said to a dog: 'Seeze rapport, Towzer!'
RAVINE	French wine: 'Ravine blonk in Paris is sensational.'
RERR	Out of this world: 'Shakespeare's a rerr writer' (once said by a Glasgow boxer trying to emulate Gene Tunney.)
RID	Red, the colour, but just to get even, 'Redd' means 'rid'. 'Get redd o it!' 'Redd oot that press!'
RONE	Roof-gutter: 'Ra baw's in ra rone' (The game's up).
SAFT	Simple, wet: 'Ah widnae say it's rainin, jiss saft a wee.'
SANNIES	Soft shoes such as plimsolls, also known as 'gutties'.
SARK	Shirt. Burns's 'Cutty Sark' meant 'Short-Shirt'.
SARKY	Sarcastic. 'Jiss don't get sarky, at's aw!'
SCUNNERT	Sickened: 'Ah'm scunnert at the haill jingbang.'
SHERIFF	Sure if: 'Ah'm sheriff ye tried ye'd manage it.'
SHIN	Shoes, soon. 'Ah'll shin fin ye a perra shin.'
SHOOGLE	Shake: 'This bus is awfy shoogly.'
SHOOIE	Hughie.
SHUCH	Ditch, muck: 'He's landit his-sel in the shuch again.'
SHUMAN	Human. A 'shuman bean' is *anthropus erectus*.
SHUMID	The condition of 'rawerra' (the climate) in Glasgow.
SKELF	A splinter, usually in the hand. 'Dinnae scart yer heid, son, ye'll get skelfs.'
SKELLY	Cross-eyed: 'It wiznae at he wiz skelly, jiss his eyes wiznae neebors.'
SMIRR	Practically raining.
SCRUFF	Neds, prigs, keelies 'nat. The lumpen proletariat as

	regarded by the proletariat.
SCUDDIES	Nudes: 'It wiz bringin in the scuddies at ruined the theayters. Noo ye jiss get thum in the Sunday papers.'
SOART	Repair, also beat-up: 'Ah kin get ye soartit, ye know.'
STEY	Reside: 'Afore ye oaffer tae tak her hame, fin oot whaur she steys!'
STOOKY	Plaster; 'stooky dolls' are the dolly shies at shows. But you hear: 'He jiss stood like a stooky.'
STRAMASH	Uproar.
STUSHIE	Much the same as stramash: 'A sterrheid stushie' is a tenement squabble.
TAEN	Taken, often used for 'took'.
TATTIES	Same as 'totties', potatoes. Both pronunciations heard.
TEWCHTER	Highlander, also performer in kilted show. A 'Tewchter bawn' is a band which plays Scottish country dance tunes, usually with accordions and drums.
THOAN	Same as 'yoan', meaning 'that over there.'
THOLE	Endure; used in Scots law — 'tholed his assizes.'
TOOK	Often used instead of 'taen' for taken. Also 'tooken'.
TRAUCHELT	Wearied physically and mentally.
WABBIT	Washed out. 'Ah'm ferr wabbit wi thae supermarkets.'
WALLIES	Dentures: 'Ye nivver weer yer wallies tae Wembley.'
WALLIE CLOSE	Tiled stair: 'Ye neednae speak Panloaf jiss because ye stey in a wallie close.'
WAN	Same as 'yin' — one; also won: 'We wan wance.'
WANES	Children (usually spelt 'weans').
WEE	Small. 'Wee haufs' get 'weer'n weer' (inflation).
WEERS	Ours, used as well as 'oors'.
WELLIES	Rubber boots, Wellingtons, made famous by Billy Connolly.
YATTER	Talk too much.
YELLAYITE	Yellowhammer; anyone wearing yellow; traffic

	warden.
YIN	Wan.
YIT	Yet. 'Ah learnt ra budgie tae say "Argentine" an' ra wee beggar's sayin it yit.'
YUCKY	Itchy.
ZAT	Is that? 'Zat you, Cherlie?'
ZEROANY	Is there any?
ZENITH	'Zenith-in wrang wi yiz?' (Is there anything wrong with you lot?)
ZINC	Does he think? 'Zinc he's oan a sure thing?'
ZION	Watching: 'He's goat zion me.'
ZLOTY	There is a lot of: 'Zloty neds oan ra coarner.'
ZONAL	Is that all? 'Zonal ye've goat?'

AWRABEST, WELL!